음원 듣기 & 단어챈트 영상

남다른 학습법으로
기적 같은 실력을 보장하는

기적의 영어리딩

체계적인 6단계 커리큘럼

	1 with 파닉스	2 with 주제 어휘	3 with 문장 패턴
목표	큰소리 리딩으로 문자 해독력을 높여요	리딩의 재미를 알며 기초 어휘력을 쌓아요	필수 문형을 접하며 문장 이해력을 높여요
리딩 소스	일상 이야기, 만화, 동화, 서사 논픽션 읽기	일상 이야기, 만화, 동화, 서사 논픽션 읽기	초대장, 포스터, 규칙 등의 정보·지식이 결합된 스토리 읽기
난이도	AR 0.5~1.0 Lexile BR~50 Words 50~70 (6p)	AR 0.7~1.5 Lexile 25~200 Words 70~90 (6p)	AR 1.3~2.3 Lexile 125~400 Words 90~110 (4p)
성취 수준	기초 어휘 180개	초등 3~4학년 교과서 수준 필수 어휘 180개	초등 5~6학년 교과서 수준 필수 어휘 200개

✓ 독해력 성장의 핵심 과정을 탄탄하게 밟아가는 6단계 리딩 프로그램

✓ 기적만의 3-Step 완전학습 시스템으로 확실한 학습 성과를 보장!

✓ 새 교육과정을 연계한 콘텐츠로 리딩 기초부터 중학 수준까지 저절로 완성!

✓ 적정 학습분량과 친절한 학습안내로 혼자서도 끝까지 완주 가능

4 with 문장 구조

다양한 글감을 읽으며 문장 구성력을 키워요
일상 소재의 실용문, 짧은 논픽션 읽기
AR 2.3~3.3 Lexile 420~620 Words 100~130
고학년 독해력 완성

5 with 문법

글을 논리적으로 이해하여 핵심을 파악해요
교과 연계된 최신 소재의 정보글 읽기
AR 3.0~3.9 Lexile 550~680 Words 130~150
예비중 리딩 · 문법 통합

6 with 서술형 영작

읽은 내용을 바탕으로 정리하는 표현력을 길러요
교과 연계된 최신 소재의 정보글, 의견글 읽기
AR 3.7~4.7 Lexile 650~780 Words 150~180
중학 독해 · 서술형 시험 대비

리딩 첫 시작부터 독해력 완성까지!

기본 다지기 — 영어와 친해지는 스토리 리딩으로 기본 바탕을 튼튼히!

Level 1 Level 2 Level 3

기적의 영어리딩 Level 1~3

- 초등 저학년의 영어 성장을 위한 리딩 기초 학습서
- 일상 이야기, 카툰, 동화 등 흥미로운 스토리로 리딩을 즐겁게 시작
- 따라가면 저절로 학습이 완성되는 3-STEP(읽기-이해-확장) 매일 학습
- 리딩의 기본기를 탄탄히 하는 파닉스 → 어휘 → 문장을 순차적으로 강화

실력 완성하기 — 논픽션 리딩으로 읽고 이해하고 표현하는 힘 기르기!

기적의 영어리딩 Level 4~6

- 초등 고학년의 문해력 완성과 중학 영어로의 연결을 돕는 리딩 심화 학습서
- 다양한 실용문과 정보글을 읽으며 글의 구조를 시각화하고 핵심을 파악하는 힘 강화
- 읽은 내용을 바탕으로 정리하고 표현하는 서술형 영작 훈련
- 문장 구조 → 논리적 이해 → 표현력 확장으로 이어지는 단계별 아웃풋 설계

p.26

monster

bed

curtains

Teddy

spider

p.29

p.42

seal

rocket

candy

monkey

p.58

bike

riding

path

Dad

p.65

p.78

story

tidy up

train

bored

soccer

p.94

moon

sun

Owls

light

Birds

p.110

stick

brick

straw

blow

p.97

1B

리딩 첫 시작
AR 0.5~1.0

기적의 영어리딩

with 파닉스

길벗스쿨

기적만의
3-Step 완전학습 시스템

읽고, 이해하고, 확장하는 3-Step 시스템으로 겉핥기가 아닌 진짜 실력을 키웁니다. 하나의 지문을 3단계에 걸쳐 깊이 있게 학습하면서 콘텐츠를 제대로 소화합니다. 동시에, 리딩의 기본 바탕이 되는 파닉스-어휘력-문장력을 차례로 강화합니다. 단순한 읽기를 넘어 문해력 성장을 위한 핵심 학습이 통합적으로 이루어지는 학습법입니다.

Step 1. 읽기

단어 익히기

스토리 지문을 이해하는 데 필수적인 키워드를 먼저 학습합니다.

스토리 리딩

몰입하여 즐길 수 있는 흥미로운 스토리를 담아, 반복하여 듣고 읽는 동안 단어와 표현을 쉽게 체화합니다.

Step 2. 이해

Step 3. 확장

내용 확인 문제

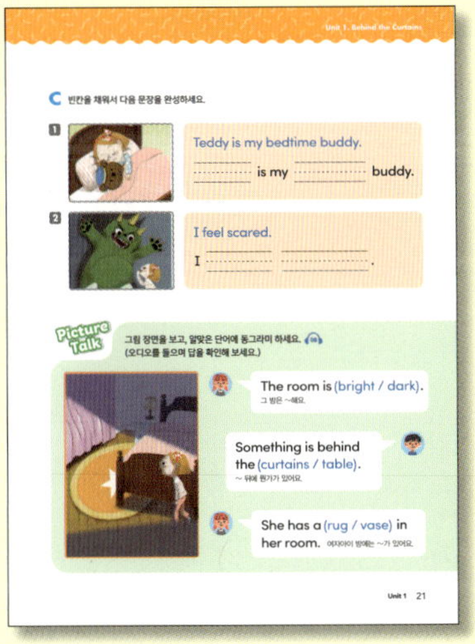

다양한 유형의 문제를 통해 읽은 내용을 충분히 이해하고, 단어 및 문장을 반복 학습하게 됩니다.

파닉스 강화

실력을 한 단계 더 끌어올리는 핵심학습을 짚고 갑니다.
Level 1에서는 문자 해독력을 높여주는 '파닉스'를 다집니다.

Contents

Level 1-B

How to Study

문자 읽기의 기초를 다지며
흥미진진한 스토리 지문으로 첫 읽기를 즐겁게 시작합니다!

Level 1은 초등 저학년 눈높이에 맞춘 쉬운 문장과 다양한 장르(일상 이야기, 동화, 만화, 서사 논픽션)를 통해 읽는 즐거움을 경험하게 합니다. Read Aloud 가이드를 따라 여러 번 듣고 큰 소리로 읽어 보세요. 읽기 유창성은 물론 콘텐츠 이해력이 빠르게 성장합니다.

더불어 라임(rime) 워드와 파닉스 어휘로 문자 학습을 다지고, 기초 어휘 108개를 확실히 익혀 리딩의 기본기를 탄탄히 쌓습니다.

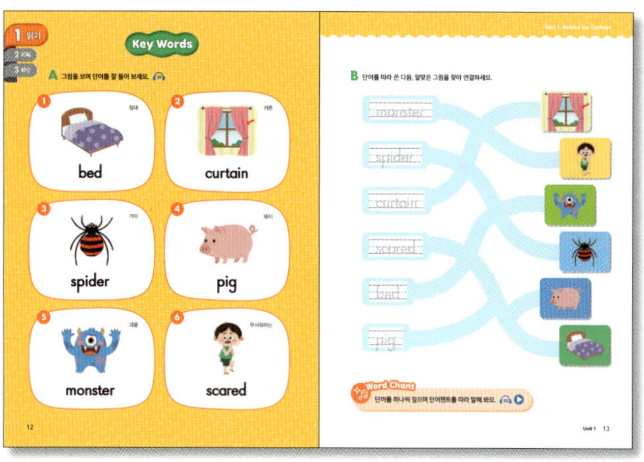

Step 1. 읽기

핵심 단어를 익힌 다음 지문 따라 읽기

❶ **[Key Words]**에서 핵심 단어의 발음을 듣고 뜻과 철자를 익혀요.

❷ 간단한 액티비티를 풀며 단어를 즐겁게 복습해요.

❸ 신나는 **[단어 챈트]**를 반복해서 들으며 단어를 확실히 익혀요.

❹ 세 가지 버전의 Read Aloud 가이드 음원을 들으며, 스토리 지문을 듣고 따라 읽어요.

[스토리 듣기] 오디오를 잘 들으며 어떤 내용인지 살펴봐요.

[집중 듣기] 손가락으로 하나씩 짚으며 글자에 집중하여 들어요.

[따라 읽기] 직접 소리내어 읽어봐요. 들려주는 문장을 한 줄씩 따라 읽어보세요.

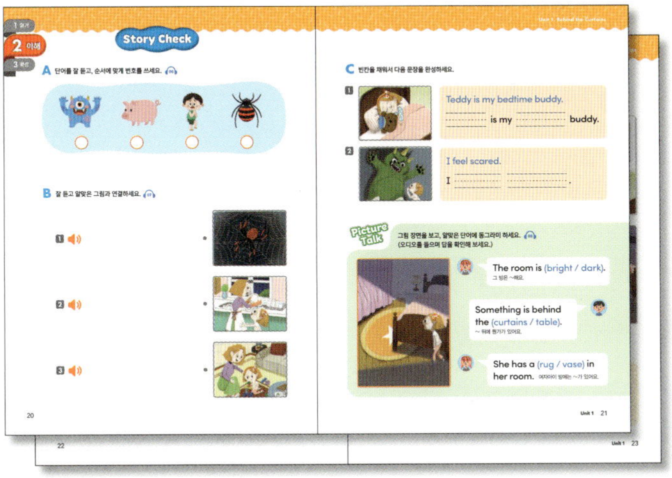

Step 2. 이해
문제를 풀며 지문을 제대로 이해하기

❶ [Story Check]에서는 여러 유형의 문제를 풀며 스토리의 흐름과 내용을 제대로 이해해요. 문제 속에서 단어와 문장을 반복해 만나며 영어표현을 자연스럽게 익혀요.

❷ 문제 풀이 후 **[별책]** 정답지를 참고하여 채점하고 틀린 문제를 확인해요.

Step 3. 확장
파닉스 점검 후, 스스로 소리내어 읽기

❶ [Phonics]에서, 스토리에 등장한 단어들의 공통 음가와 철자를 확인해요.

❷ 공통 음가끼리 분류하는 문제와 낯선 단어를 읽어보는 [Challenge] 코너로 파닉스를 강화해요.

❸ [I Can Read] 스스로 소리 내어 읽기 연습을 해요. 직접 소리내서 읽을수록 리딩 실력이 좋아집니다.

[Review Test] 리뷰 테스트 2회분이 포함됩니다. Unit 1~3에 대한 테스트와 Unit 4~6에 대한 테스트로 영어 실력을 확인해 볼 수 있어요.

[별책: Practice Book] 단어, 문장, 파닉스, 딕테이션에 관련해 선택적으로 보충학습을 할 수 있습니다.

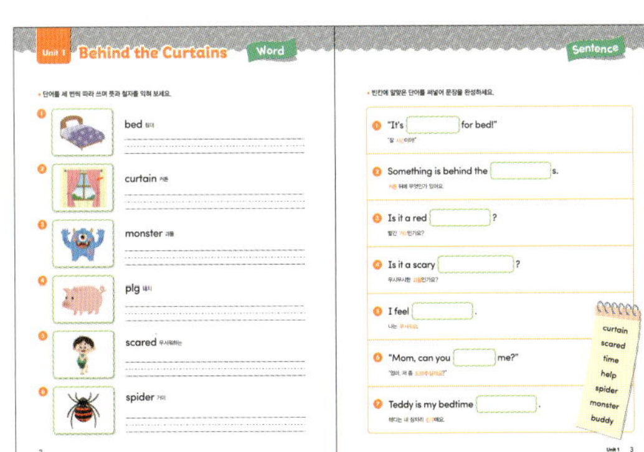

Study Plan

학습 완주를 위해 미리 학습계획을 세워 보세요.
주 5일 학습하여 한 달 완성하기, 또는 주 3일 학습하여 6주 완성하기!
나에게 맞는 계획은 어느 쪽인가요? 목표를 세운 다음, 아래 진도표를 따라 공부해 보세요.

주 5일 학습 스케줄

4 Week

Week 1	**Unit 1**	**Unit 1**	**Unit 1**	**Unit 2**	**Unit 2**
	Step 1 읽기 본책 p.12~19 별책 p.2	**Step 2** 이해 본책 p.20~23 별책 p.3	**Step 3** 확장 본책 p.24~26 별책 p.4~5	**Step 1** 읽기 본책 p.28~35 별책 p.6	**Step 2** 이해 본책 p.36~39 별책 p.7
	◯월◯일	◯월◯일	◯월◯일	◯월◯일	◯월◯일
Week 2	**Unit 2**	**Unit 3**	**Unit 3**	**Unit 3**	**Review Test 1**
	Step 3 확장 본책 p.40~42 별책 p.8~9	**Step 1** 읽기 본책 p.44~51 별책 p.10	**Step 2** 이해 본책 p.52~55 별책 p.11	**Step 3** 확장 본책 p.56~58 별책 p.12~13	본책 p.59~62
	◯월◯일	◯월◯일	◯월◯일	◯월◯일	◯월◯일
Week 3	**Unit 4**	**Unit 4**	**Unit 4**	**Unit 5**	**Unit 5**
	Step 1 읽기 본책 p.64~71 별책 p.14	**Step 2** 이해 본책 p.72~75 별책 p.15	**Step 3** 확장 본책 p.76~78 별책 p.16~17	**Step 1** 읽기 본책 p.80~87 별책 p.18	**Step 2** 이해 본책 p.88~91 별책 p.19
	◯월◯일	◯월◯일	◯월◯일	◯월◯일	◯월◯일
Week 4	**Unit 5**	**Unit 6**	**Unit 6**	**Unit 6**	**Review Test 2**
	Step 3 확장 본책 p.92~94 별책 p.20~21	**Step 1** 읽기 본책 p.96~103 별책 p.22	**Step 2** 이해 본책 p.104~107 별책 p.23	**Step 3** 확장 본책 p.108~110 별책 p.24~25	본책 p.111~114
	◯월◯일	◯월◯일	◯월◯일	◯월◯일	◯월◯일

6 Week

주 3일 학습 스케줄

Week 1 Unit 1	Step 1 읽기 본책 p.12~19 별책 p.2	Step 2 이해 본책 p.20~23 별책 p.3	Step 3 확장 본책 p.24~26 별책 p.4~5	
	◯월◯일	◯월◯일	◯월◯일	
Week 2 Unit 2	Step 1 읽기 본책 p.28~35 별책 p.6	Step 2 이해 본책 p.36~39 별책 p.7	Step 3 확장 본책 p.40~42 별책 p.8~9	
	◯월◯일	◯월◯일	◯월◯일	
Week 3 Unit 3	Step 1 읽기 본책 p.44~51 별책 p.10	Step 2 이해 본책 p.52~55 별책 p.11	Step 3 확장 본책 p.56~58 별책 p.12~13	Review Test 1 본책 p.59~62
	◯월◯일	◯월◯일	◯월◯일	◯월◯일
Week 4 Unit 4	Step 1 읽기 본책 p.64~71 별책 p.14	Step 2 이해 본책 p.72~75 별책 p.15	Step 3 확장 본책 p.76~78 별책 p.16~17	
	◯월◯일	◯월◯일	◯월◯일	
Week 5 Unit 5	Step 1 읽기 본책 p.80~87 별책 p.18	Step 2 이해 본책 p.88~91 별책 p.19	Step 3 확장 본책 p.92~94 별책 p.20~21	
	◯월◯일	◯월◯일	◯월◯일	
Week 6 Unit 6	Step 1 읽기 본책 p.96~103 별책 p.22	Step 2 이해 본책 p.104~107 별책 p.23	Step 3 확장 본책 p.108~110 별책 p.24~25	Review Test 2 본책 p.111~114
	◯월◯일	◯월◯일	◯월◯일	◯월◯일

Read Aloud를 위한 4가지 음원

- 읽기 준비를 위한 [단어 챈트]
- 그림과 함께 [스토리 듣기]
- 글자를 짚으며 [집중 듣기]
- 한 문장씩 [따라 읽기]

길벗스쿨 e클래스 에서 오디오 바로 듣기

eclass.gilbut.co.kr에서 학습에 필요한
모든 음원를 제공합니다.
오디오 번호를 찾아 한 번만 탭하면
단어와 스토리를 바로 들을 수 있어요.

학습의 재미를 더하는 스티커 활동!

그림 스티커를 붙이며 단어·문장을 익혀요.

Unit

1

Behind the Curtains

STEP 1 읽기	STEP 2 이해	STEP 3 확장
핵심 단어를 익혀서 스토리 듣고 읽기	읽은 내용을 점검하며 스토리 이해하기	파닉스를 강화하여 유창하게 읽기

Key Words

A 그림을 보며 단어를 잘 들어 보세요. 01

1 침대

bed

2 커튼

curtain

3 거미

spider

4 돼지

pig

5 괴물

monster

6 무서워하는

scared

B 단어를 따라 쓴 다음, 알맞은 그림을 찾아 연결하세요.

monster

spider

curtain

scared

bed

pig

Word Chant

단어를 하나씩 짚으며 단어챈트를 따라 말해 봐요. 02

Behind the Curtains

"It's time for bed!"

Look!

Something is behind the curtains.

What could it be?

Is it a red spider?

Is it a big pig?

Is it a scary monster?

I feel scared.

"Mom, can you help me?"

"Let's check together. One, two, three – look!"

Oh,
it's Teddy!

Teddy is my
bedtime buddy.

Story Check

A 단어를 잘 듣고, 순서에 맞게 번호를 쓰세요. 06

B 잘 듣고 알맞은 그림과 연결하세요. 07

1

2

3

C 빈칸을 채워서 다음 문장을 완성하세요.

1

Teddy is my bedtime buddy.

__________ is my __________ buddy.

2

I feel scared.

I __________ __________.

Picture Talk

그림 장면을 보고, 알맞은 단어에 동그라미 하세요. 08
(오디오를 들으며 답을 확인해 보세요.)

The room is (bright / dark).
그 방은 ~해요.

Something is behind the (curtains / table).
~ 뒤에 뭔가가 있어요.

She has a (rug / vase) in her room. 여자아이 방에는 ~가 있어요.

D 주인공 소녀가 커튼 뒤에 있다고 상상한 것은 무엇이었나요? 어떤 특징을 가졌는지 연결하세요.

 • • big • • spider

 • • scary • • monster

 • • red • • pig

E 커튼 뒤에 있던 것을 찾아 동그라미 하세요.

What is behind the curtains?

F 스토리를 다시 들으며 이야기 순서에 맞게 번호를 쓰세요. 09

( ) 

( ) 

( ) 

( ) 

( ) 

( ) 

Think & Say

잠잘 때 항상 곁을 지켜주는 잠자리 친구가 있나요? 이름도 지어줬나요?

여러분의 Bedtime Buddy를 소개해 보세요!

__________ is my bedtime buddy!

Phonics

A 단어를 듣고 따라 말해 보세요. 그다음, 빈곳에 알맞은 철자를 쓰세요. 10

1

bed → b / ___

2

red → r / ___

3

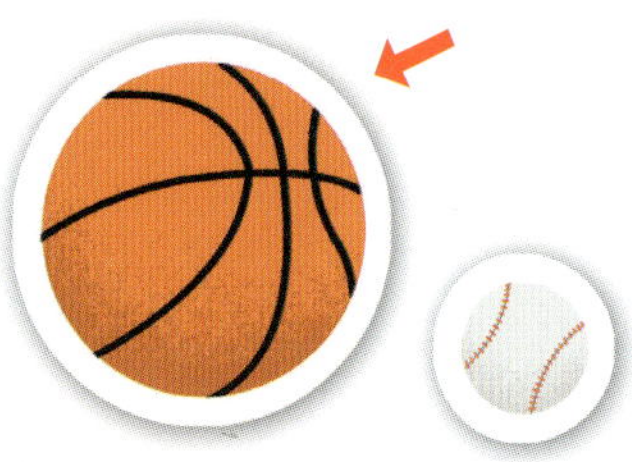

big → b / ___

4

pig → p / ___

5

Teddy → Ted / ___

6

buddy → bud / ___

B 같은 소리가 나는 단어끼리 모아 알맞은 곳에 쓰세요.

red Teddy big

buddy pig bed

-ig

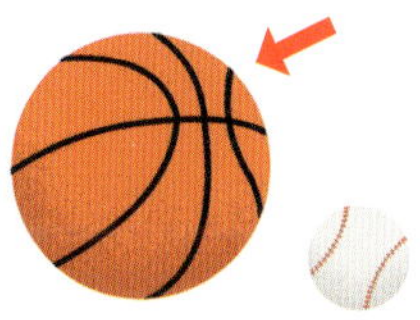

-ed

-dy

Challenge

새로운 단어도 스스로 읽을 수 있나요? 오디오를 들으며 확인해 보세요. 11

sled — Yes ☐ No ☐

dig — Yes ☐ No ☐

daddy — Yes ☐ No ☐

I Can Read

Behind the Curtains

"It's time for ______ !"

Look!
Something is behind the ______ .
What could it be?

Is it a red ______ ?
Is it a big pig?

Is it a scary ______ ?
I feel scared.

"Mom, can you help me?"
"Let's check together.
One, two, three - look!"

Oh, it's ______ !
Teddy is my bedtime buddy.

Self-Check

- ☐ 스토리 전체를 스스로 읽을 수 있어요.
- ☐ 배운 단어의 뜻을 잘 알아요.
- ☐ 헷갈리는 발음은 다시 들으며 확실히 익혔어요.

단어 스티커를 붙여 글을 완성하고 큰 소리로 읽어 보세요.
스토리를 다시 들으며 잘 읽었는지 확인해 보세요. 12

Unit
2

My Amazing Dad

STEP 1 읽기	STEP 2 이해	STEP 3 확장
핵심 단어를 익혀서 스토리 듣고 읽기	읽은 내용을 점검하며 스토리 이해하기	파닉스를 강화하여 유창하게 읽기

Key Words

A 그림을 보며 단어를 잘 들어 보세요. 13

1

사탕

candy

2

들어 올리다

lift

3

원숭이

monkey

4

빠른

fast

5

로켓

rocket

6

물개

seal

B 그림 스티커를 붙여서 액자를 완성한 다음, 단어를 따라 쓰세요.

seal

rocket

lift

candy

monkey

fast

Word Chant

단어를 하나씩 짚으며 단어챈트를 따라 말해 봐요. 14

My Amazing Dad

Dad is sweet like candy.
He gives me a big hug.

Dad is strong like a bear.

He can lift me up high!

Dad is funny like a monkey.
He can make a funny face.

Dad is fast like a rocket.
He wins every race.

Dad is cool like a seal.
He can swim in the sea.

I love my dad so much.

He is the best!

Story Check

A 단어를 잘 듣고, 순서에 맞게 번호를 쓰세요. 18

B 잘 듣고 알맞은 그림과 연결하세요. 19

1

2

3

C 빈칸을 채워서 다음 문장을 완성하세요.

1

He can lift me up high!

He can ________ me up ________!

2

Dad is cool like a seal.

Dad is ________ like a ________.

Picture Talk

그림 장면을 보고, 질문에 알맞은 대답을 완성하세요. 20
(오디오를 들으며 답을 확인해 보세요.)

Who wins the race?
(누가 경기에서 이기나요?)

________ wins the race.
(~가 경기에서 이겨요.)

Dad is ________ like a rocket. (아빠는 로켓처럼 ~해요.)

funny fast Dad Mom

D 주인공 소녀는 아빠를 무엇에 비유했나요? 알맞게 연결하세요.

Dad is …

sweet

funny

strong

fast

cool

like a monkey

like candy

like a bear

like a seal

like a rocket

E 스토리를 다시 들으며 이야기 순서에 맞게 번호를 쓰세요. 21

Think & Say

우리 가족은 어떤 동물이나 사물을 닮았다고 할 수 있을까요? 가족 한 사람을 떠올려 특징을 말해 보세요.

My ________ is ________ like a ________.

Phonics

A 단어를 듣고 따라 말해 보세요. 그다음, 빈곳에 알맞은 철자를 쓰세요. 22

1

race → r ___

2

face → f ___

3

seal → s ___ l

4

sea → s ___

5

fast → fa ___

6

best → be ___

B 같은 소리가 나는 단어끼리 모아 알맞은 곳에 쓰세요.

face　seal　best
sea　fast　race

-st

____

____

-ace

____

____

-ea-

____

____

challenge 새로운 단어도 스스로 읽을 수 있나요? 오디오를 들으며 확인해 보세요. 23

lace　Yes ☐　No ☐

read　Yes ☐　No ☐

nest　Yes ☐　No ☐

I Can Read

My Amazing Dad

Dad is sweet like 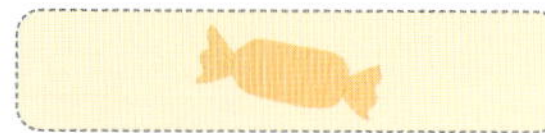.
He gives me a big hug.

Dad is strong like a bear.
He can lift me up high!

Dad is funny like a .
He can make a funny face.

Dad is fast like a .
He wins every race.

Dad is cool like a .
He can swim in the sea.

I love my dad so much.
He is the best!

Self-Check

- [ ] 스토리 전체를 스스로 읽을 수 있어요.
- [ ] 배운 단어의 뜻을 잘 알아요.
- [ ] 헷갈리는 발음은 다시 들으며 확실히 익혔어요.

단어 스티커를 붙여 글을 완성하고 큰 소리로 읽어 보세요.
스토리를 다시 들으며 잘 읽었는지 확인해 보세요. 24

Unit

3

My First Ride

STEP 1 읽기
핵심 단어를 익혀서
스토리 듣고 읽기

STEP 2 이해
읽은 내용을 점검하며
스토리 이해하기

STEP 3 확장
파닉스를 강화하여
유창하게 읽기

1 읽기
2 이해
3 확장

Key Words

A 그림을 보며 단어를 잘 들어 보세요. 25

1

새, 새로 산

new

2

자전거

bike

3

(자전거 등을) 타다, 타기

ride

4

길

path

5

(손으로) 잡고 있다

hold

6

큰 소리로 말하다, 외치다

shout

B 단어를 따라 쓴 다음, 알맞은 그림을 찾아 연결하세요.

path

bike

hold

ride

shout

new

Word Chant

단어를 하나씩 짚으며 단어챈트를 따라 말해 봐요. 26

My First Ride

I have a shiny new bike.
It's a birthday gift from Dad.

We get our bikes.
Dad will help me ride.
We're both excited.

The path is wide.
I feel a little nervous.

"Hold on tight for me,"
I say.

"Okay," Dad says.

"Are you still holding on?"
I shout.

I look back.
I'm riding all by myself!

Story Check

A 단어를 잘 듣고, 순서에 맞게 번호를 쓰세요. 30

B 잘 듣고 알맞은 그림과 연결하세요. 31

1

2

3

C 빈칸을 채워서 다음 문장을 완성하세요.

1

Are you still holding on?

Are you ________ ________ on?

2

I'm riding all by myself!

I'm ________ all by ________!

Picture Talk

그림 장면을 보고, 알맞은 단어에 동그라미 하세요. 32
(오디오를 들으며 답을 확인해 보세요.)

Dad (is / is not) holding the bike. 아빠는 자전거를 ~고 있어요.

The path is (wide / shiny). 길은 ~해요.

The boy is (sad / nervous). 소년은 ~해요.

D 주인공 소년이 혼자서 자전거를 타게 되는 과정에서 느낀 감정을 알맞게 연결하세요.

I feel nervous.

I'm excited.

I feel proud.

*proud 자랑스러운

E 다음을 읽고 옳으면 Yes, 틀리면 No에 V표 하세요.

	Yes	No
Mom will help me ride.	☐	☐
I have a new bike.	☐	☐

F 스토리를 다시 들으며 이야기 순서에 맞게 번호를 쓰세요. 33

Think & Say

도움 없이 내가 스스로 할 수 있는
일이 무엇인지 생각해 보고,
자신있게 말해 봐요.

Phonics

A 단어를 듣고 따라 말해 보세요. 그다음, 빈곳에 알맞은 철자를 쓰세요. 34

1

ride → r / ____

2

wide → w / ____

3

path → pa / ____

4

both → bo / ____

5

shiny → ____ / iny

6

shout → ____ / out

B 같은 소리가 나는 단어끼리 모아 알맞은 곳에 쓰세요.

both　wide　shout
ride　shiny　path

sh-

-th

-ide

challenge

새로운 단어도 스스로 읽을 수 있나요? 오디오를 들으며 확인해 보세요. 35

hide　Yes ☐　No ☐

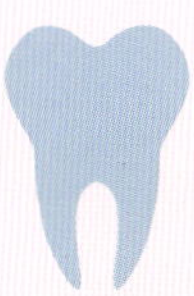

tooth　Yes ☐　No ☐

ship　Yes ☐　No ☐

I Can Read

My First Ride

I have a shiny new ______ .
It's a birthday gift from Dad.

We get our bikes.
______ will help me ride.
We're both excited.

The ______ is wide.
I feel a little nervous.

"Hold on tight for me," I say.
"Okay," Dad says.

"Are you still holding on?" I shout.

I look back.
I'm ______ all by myself!

Self-Check

- ☐ 스토리 전체를 스스로 읽을 수 있어요.
- ☐ 배운 단어의 뜻을 잘 알아요.
- ☐ 헷갈리는 발음은 다시 들으며 확실히 익혔어요.

단어 스티커를 붙여 글을 완성하고 큰 소리로 읽어 보세요.
스토리를 다시 들으며 잘 읽었는지 확인해 보세요. 36

Review Test ❶

Words 그림을 보고 알맞은 단어에 V 표시를 하세요. / 10

1 
☐ seal
☐ monkey

2 
☐ bed
☐ curtain

3 
☐ sea
☐ path

4 
☐ rocket
☐ bike

5 
☐ bear
☐ pig

6 
☐ old
☐ new

7 
☐ monster
☐ spider

8 
☐ wide
☐ fast

9 
☐ hold
☐ ride

10 
☐ bike
☐ box

Comprehension A 다음을 읽고 알맞은 그림에 V 표시를 하세요.

/ 6

1 sweet like candy

☐ 

☐ 

2 a scary monster

☐ 

☐ 

3 behind the curtains

☐ 

☐ 

4 a shiny new bike

☐ 

☐ 

5 make a funny face

☐ 

☐ 

6 help me ride

☐ 

☐ 

Comprehension B 빈칸에 들어갈 알맞은 단어에 V 표시를 하세요.

/ 5

1 

We're both ______________.

☐ excited ☐ nervous

2 

Dad is funny like a __________.

☐ seal ☐ monkey

3 

The __________ is wide.

☐ bike ☐ path

4 

Teddy is my bedtime __________.

☐ daddy ☐ buddy

5 

Dad can __________ me up high!

☐ lift ☐ swim

정답 ▶ 별책 p.40

Phonics 단어를 잘 듣고 알맞은 것에 동그라미 한 뒤, 그림과 연결하세요. 37

/ 8

1 race / face

2 red / bed

3 best / fast

4 ride / wide

5 path / both

6 buddy / Teddy

7 shout / shiny

8 pig / big

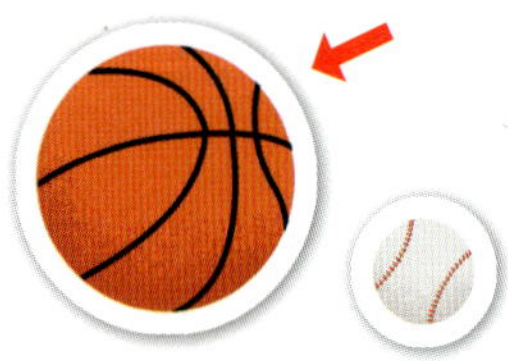

Unit

4

Maybe Next Time!

STEP 1 읽기	STEP 2 이해	STEP 3 확장
핵심 단어를 익혀서 스토리 듣고 읽기	읽은 내용을 점검하며 스토리 이해하기	파닉스를 강화하여 유창하게 읽기

Key Words

A 그림을 보며 단어를 잘 들어 보세요. 38

1

지루해하는

bored

2

놀다

play

3

읽다,
읽어주다

read

4

아프다

hurt

5

엉망인 상태

mess

6

~을 정리하다

tidy up

B 그림 스티커를 붙여서 액자를 완성한 다음, 단어를 따라 쓰세요.

sticker

read

sticker

play

sticker

bored

sticker

mess

sticker

tidy up

sticker

hurt

Word Chant

단어를 하나씩 짚으며 단어챈트를 따라 말해 봐요. 39

Maybe Next Time!

Let's play soccer,
Dad.
I guess it's going to rain.
Maybe next time!

Read me a story, Mom.
My head hurts. Maybe next time!
RABBIT

Ta-da! I have slime and a train.
Maybe next time!

Fine, I'll just play all by myself.
What a mess!
It's time to tidy up!

Maybe next time!

Story Check

A 단어를 잘 듣고, 순서에 맞게 번호를 쓰세요. 43

B 잘 듣고 알맞은 그림과 연결하세요. 44

1

2

3

C 빈칸에 들어갈 알맞은 말을 찾아 V 표시를 하세요.

1

I'm ____________.

☐ angry ☐ bored

2

It's time to ________ up!

☐ tidy ☐ make

Picture Talk

그림 장면을 보고, 다음 대화를 완성하세요. 45
(오디오를 들으며 답을 확인해 보세요.)

The boy wants to play ____________. (소년은 ~를 하고 싶어요.)

But he can't. Why not?
(하지만 그럴 수 없어요. 왜 안될까요?)

Because it's going to ____________.
(왜냐하면 ~할 것이기 때문이에요.)

snow rain soccer

He wants to ...

D 주인공 소년은 누구와 무엇을 하고 싶었나요?

play soccer

play with toys

read a story

E 가족들은 주인공 소년에게 뭐라고 답했나요?

Maybe next time!

Sure. Let's have fun.

F 스토리를 다시 들으며 이야기 순서에 맞게 번호를 쓰세요. 46

Think & Say

심심할 때는 재미있는 일을 하고 싶어지죠.
이럴 땐 친구나 가족에게 'I want to ~'를
써서 무얼 하고 싶은지 말해 보세요.

I want to
______________!

Phonics

A 단어를 듣고 따라 말해 보세요. 그다음, 빈곳에 알맞은 철자를 쓰세요. 47

1

time → t / ______

2

slime → sl / ______

3

rain → r / ______

4

train → tr / ______

5

guess → gu / ______

6

mess → m / ______

B 같은 소리가 나는 단어끼리 모아 알맞은 곳에 쓰세요.

time　rain　guess
train　mess　slime

-ess

-ime

-ain

Challenge

새로운 단어도 스스로 읽을 수 있나요? 오디오를 들으며 확인해 보세요. 48

lime　Yes □　No □

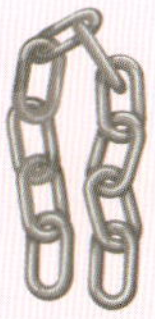

chain　Yes □　No □

dress　Yes □　No □

I Can Read

Maybe Next Time

I'm ______ .
I want to play.

Let's play ______ , Dad.
I guess it's going to rain.
Maybe next time!

Read me a ______ , Mom.
My head hurts.
Maybe next time!

Ta-da! I have slime and a ______ .
Maybe next time!

Fine, I'll just play all by myself.

What a mess!
It's time to ______ !
Maybe next time!

Self-Check

- ☐ 스토리 전체를 스스로 읽을 수 있어요.
- ☐ 배운 단어의 뜻을 잘 알아요.
- ☐ 헷갈리는 발음은 다시 들으며 확실히 익혔어요.

단어 스티커를 붙여 글을 완성하고 큰 소리로 읽어 보세요.
스토리를 다시 들으며 잘 읽었는지 확인해 보세요. 49

Unit

5

Day and Night

STEP 1 읽기	STEP 2 이해	STEP 3 확장
핵심 단어를 익혀서 스토리 듣고 읽기	읽은 내용을 점검하며 스토리 이해하기	파닉스를 강화하여 유창하게 읽기

Key Words

A 그림을 보며 단어를 잘 들어 보세요. 50

1

아침
morning

2

(잠에서) 깨다, 깨우다
wake up

3

밤
night

4

(잠을) 자다
sleep

5

(전기 등을) 끄다
turn off

6

올빼미
owl

B 단어를 따라 쓴 다음, 알맞은 그림을 찾아 연결하세요.

wake up

night

turn off

owl

morning

sleep

Word Chant

단어를 하나씩 짚으며 단어챈트를 따라 말해 봐요. 51

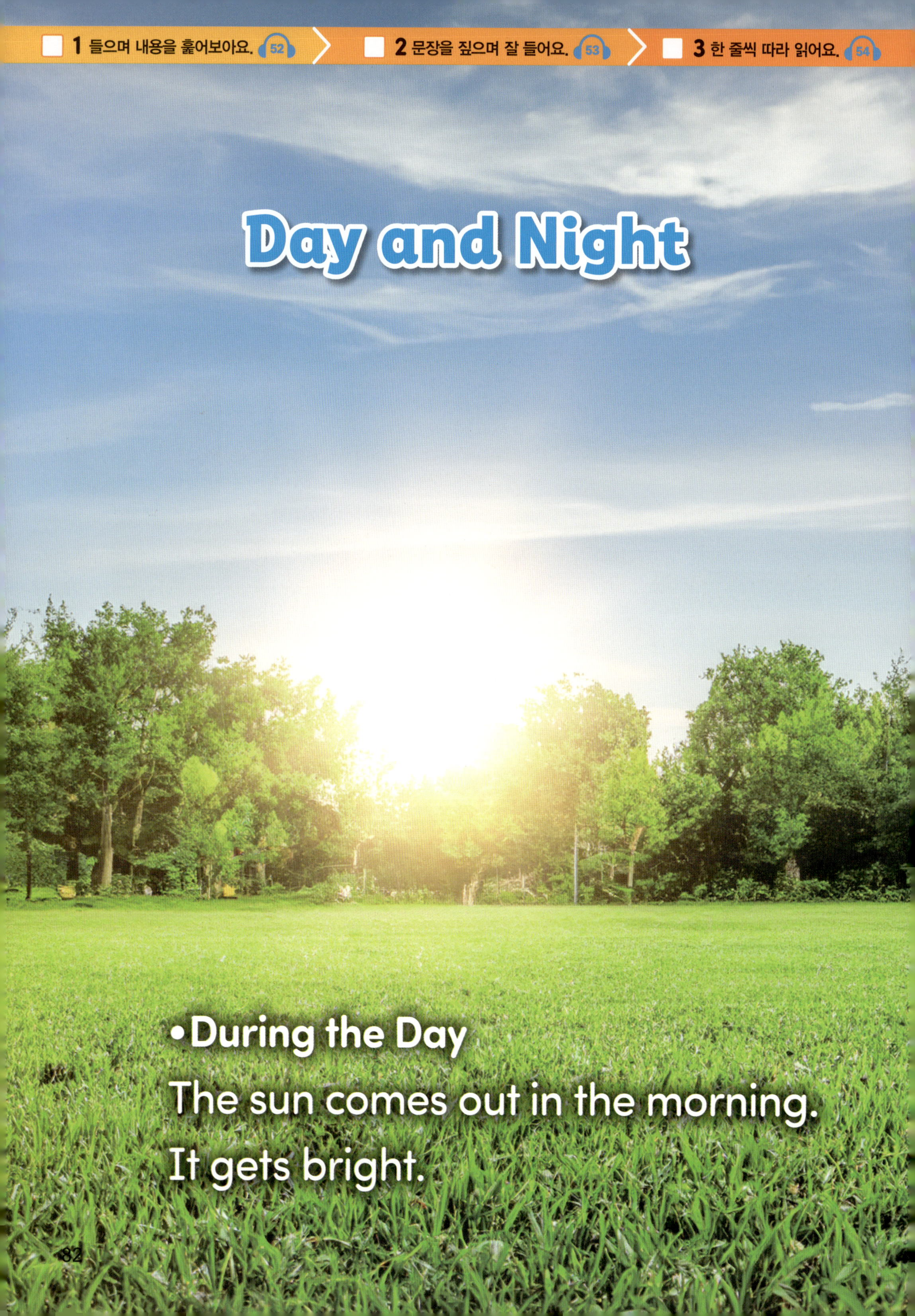

Day and Night

• During the Day

The sun comes out in the morning.
It gets bright.

Birds wake me up.

Dad goes to work.
I go to school.

•At Night

The moon comes out at night.
It gets dark.

Ben goes to sleep.

And I go to sleep, too.
I turn off the light.

Owls hoot at night.
Aren't you sleepy, Mr. Owl?

Story Check

A 단어를 잘 듣고, 순서에 맞게 번호를 쓰세요. 55

B 잘 듣고 알맞은 그림과 연결하세요. 56

1

2

3

C 빈칸을 채워서 다음 문장을 완성하세요.

1

Birds wake me up.

Birds ________ me ________.

2

I turn off the light.

I ________ ________ the light.

Picture Talk

그림 장면을 보고, 질문에 알맞은 대답을 완성하세요. 57
(오디오를 들으며 답을 확인해 보세요.)

Who doesn't sleep at night?
누가 밤에 잠을 자지 않나요?

Mr. ________ doesn't sleep at night. ~가 밤에 잠을 자지 않아요.

girl dog Owl

D 낮과 밤의 모습은 어떠한가요? 어색한 그림을 찾아 X표를 하세요.

During the Day

sun

bird

bright

sleep

work

At Night

moon

owl

dark

turn off

wake up

E 스토리를 다시 들으며 이야기 순서에 맞게 번호를 쓰세요. 58

Think & Say

주인공은 새 소리에 아침 잠을 깨요.

여러분의 아침 잠은 누가 깨우나요?

_________ wakes me up in the morning!

1 읽기
2 이해
3 확장

Phonics

A 단어를 듣고 따라 말해 보세요. 그다음, 빈곳에 알맞은 철자를 쓰세요. 59

1 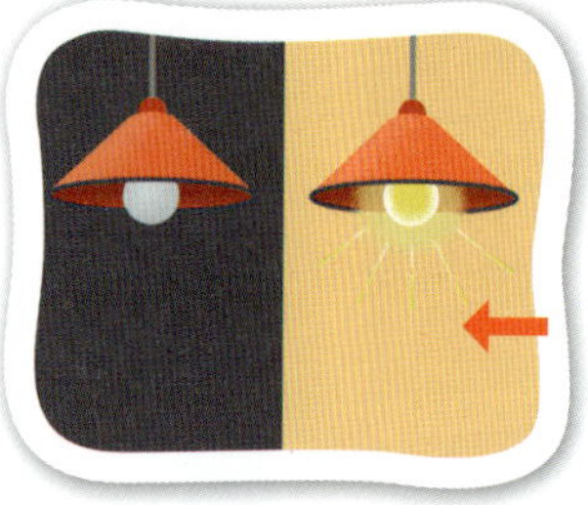

bright → br ___

2 

night → n ___

3 

light → l ___

4 

school → sch ___ l

5 

spoon → sp ___ n

6 

moon → m ___ n

B 단어를 읽으며 따라 쓴 다음, 알맞은 그림을 찾아 번호를 쓰세요.

-oo-

spoon •	• 

school •	• 

moon •	• 

-ight

light •	• 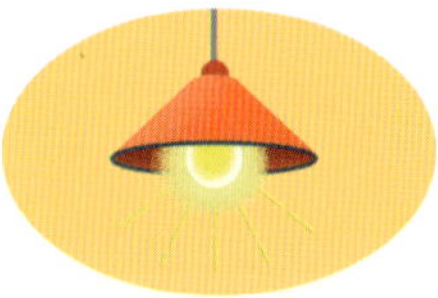

bright •	• 

night •	• 

challenge

새로운 단어도 스스로 읽을 수 있나요? 오디오를 들으며 확인해 보세요. 60

fight

Yes ☐

No ☐

food

Yes ☐

No ☐

I Can Read

Day and Night

•During the Day

The [sticker] comes out in the morning.
It gets bright.

"Tweet, tweet!" [sticker] wake me up.

Dad goes to work.
I go to school.

•At Night

The [sticker] comes out at night.
It gets dark.

Ben goes to sleep.
And I go to sleep, too.
I turn off the [sticker] .

"Hoot, hoot!" [sticker] hoot at night.
Aren't you sleepy, Mr. Owl?

단어 스티커를 붙여 글을 완성하고 큰 소리로 읽어 보세요.
스토리를 다시 들으며 잘 읽었는지 확인해 보세요. 61

Self-Check

- ☐ 스토리 전체를 스스로 읽을 수 있어요.
- ☐ 배운 단어의 뜻을 잘 알아요.
- ☐ 헷갈리는 발음은 다시 들으며 확실히 익혔어요.

Unit 6

The Three Little Pigs

STEP 1 읽기	STEP 2 이해	STEP 3 확장
핵심 단어를 익혀서 스토리 듣고 읽기	읽은 내용을 점검하며 스토리 이해하기	파닉스를 강화하여 유창하게 읽기

Key Words

A 그림을 보며 단어를 잘 들어 보세요. 62

1 (건물을) 짓다

build

2 짚, 지푸라기

straw

3 집

house

4 나뭇가지, 막대기

stick

5 벽돌

brick

6 (입으로) 불다

blow

B 그림 스티커를 붙여서 액자를 완성한 다음, 단어를 따라 쓰세요.

straw

build

stick

brick

blow

house

Word Chant

단어를 하나씩 짚으며 단어챈트를 따라 말해 봐요. 63

☐ **1** 들으며 내용을 훑어보아요. 64 ☐ **2** 문장을 짚으며 잘 들어요. 65 ☐ **3** 한 줄씩 따라 읽어요. 66

The Three Little Pigs

The three little pigs live in a town.
"We're great builders," they say.

The first pig builds a straw house.

The second pig builds a stick house.

The third pig builds a brick house.

It is thick and strong.

“Knock, knock!
Let me in.”

The wolf blows the straw house away.

"Knock, knock!
Let me in."

The wolf blows the stick house away.

The wolf cannot blow
the brick house down.

The three little pigs
dance in the dirt and dust.

Story Check

A 단어를 잘 듣고, 순서에 맞게 번호를 쓰세요. 67

 ○

 ○

 ○

 ○

B 잘 듣고 알맞은 그림과 연결하세요. 68

1 🔊 • 

2 🔊 • 

3 🔊 • 

C 빈칸에 들어갈 알맞은 말을 찾아 V 표시를 하세요.

1

The first pig builds a ________ house.

☐ straw ☐ brick

2

The wolf ________s the stick house away.

☐ build ☐ blow

Picture Talk

그림 장면을 보고, 알맞은 단어에 동그라미 하세요. 69
(오디오를 들으며 답을 확인해 보세요.)

The wolf cannot blow the (stick / brick) house down.
늑대는 ~집을 불어 무너뜨리지 못해요.

Why not?

The brick house is thick and (strong / soft).
벽돌집은 두껍고 ~해요.

D 돼지 삼형제는 각각 어떤 집을 짓나요? 사다리를 타고 내려가 번호를 쓰고, 문장을 완성하세요.

The ________ pig builds a ________ house.

E 스토리를 다시 들으며 이야기 순서에 맞게 번호를 쓰세요. 70

Think & Say

여러분이 동화 속 주인공이라면 어떤 집을
지고 싶나요? 무엇으로 집을 짓고 싶은지
말해 보세요.

I will build a
__________ house!

Phonics

A 단어를 듣고 따라 말해 보세요. 그다음, 빈곳에 알맞은 철자를 쓰세요. 71

1

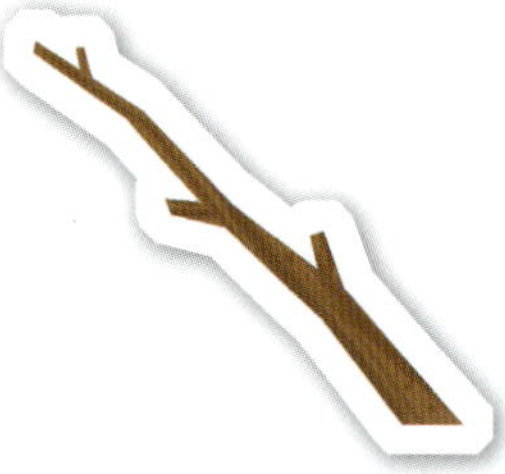

stick → st ___

2

brick → br ___

3

thick → th ___

4

third → th ___ d

5

first → f ___ st

6

dirt → d ___ t

B 단어를 읽으며 따라 쓴 다음, 알맞은 그림을 찾아 번호를 쓰세요.

-ick

( ) thick

( ) brick

( ) stick

-ir-

( ) dirt

( ) first

( ) third

1

2

3

4

5
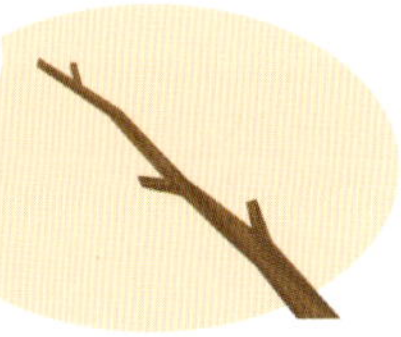

6

challenge 새로운 단어도 스스로 읽을 수 있나요? 오디오를 들으며 확인해 보세요. 72

kick

Yes ☐

No ☐

girl

Yes ☐

No ☐

I Can Read

The Three Little Pigs

The three little pigs live in a town.
"We're great builders," they say.

The first pig builds a [ ] house.
The second pig builds a stick house.

The third pig builds a [ ] house.
It is thick and strong.

"Knock, knock! Let me in."
The wolf blows the straw house away.

"Knock, knock! Let me in."
The wolf blows the [ ] house away.

The wolf cannot [ ]
the brick house down.
The three little pigs dance
in the dirt and dust.

Self-Check

- [ ] 스토리 전체를 스스로 읽을 수 있어요.
- [ ] 배운 단어의 뜻을 잘 알아요.
- [ ] 헷갈리는 발음은 다시 들으며 확실히 익혔어요.

단어 스티커를 붙여 글을 완성하고 큰 소리로 읽어 보세요.
스토리를 다시 들으며 잘 읽었는지 확인해 보세요. 73

Review Test ❷

Words 그림을 보고 알맞은 단어에 V 표시를 하세요.

/ 10

1

- ☐ mess
- ☐ dust

2

- ☐ house
- ☐ train

3

- ☐ sleep
- ☐ wake up

4

- ☐ turn off
- ☐ tidy up

5

- ☐ brick
- ☐ stick

6

- ☐ read
- ☐ hurt

7

- ☐ blow
- ☐ play

8

- ☐ wake up
- ☐ sleep

9

- ☐ morning
- ☐ night

10

- ☐ stick
- ☐ straw

Comprehension A 다음을 읽고 알맞은 그림에 V 표시를 하세요.

/ 6

1 turn off the light

2 a stick house

3 blow away

4 I'm bored.

5 It gets dark.

6 go to sleep

Comprehension B 빈칸에 들어갈 알맞은 단어에 V 표시를 하세요.

/ 5

1 

_________ hoot at night.

☐ Pigs ☐ Owls

2 

The first pig _________ a straw house.

☐ builds ☐ blows

3 

"Let's _________ soccer."

☐ read ☐ play

4 

"My _________ hurts."

☐ eyes ☐ head

5 

"What a _________!"

☐ clean ☐ mess

정답 ▶ 별책 p.40

Phonics 단어를 잘 듣고 알맞은 것에 동그라미 한 뒤, 그림과 연결하세요. 74

/ 8

1 rain / train

2 stick / brick

3 time / slime

4 thick / stick

5 night / light

6 school / spoon

7 mess / guess

8 dirt / third

NICE WORK

저자 C2 Archive (대표 Olene Kim)

지난 20여 년간 영어라는 언어를 어린이들이 어려움 없이 단계적으로 습득해갈 수 있도록 효과적인 교수법을 연구하여 다양한 교재로 구현해 온 영어교육 전문 집필진입니다. 파닉스, 리딩, 코스북, 문법 등 여러 분야의 ELT 교재와 영어 단행본 학습서를 집필·개발하였습니다.

저자 기적학습연구소

"혼자서 작은 산을 넘는 아이가 나중에 큰 산도 넘습니다." 본 연구소는 아이들이 혼자서 큰 산까지 넘을 수 있는 힘을 키워주고자 합니다. 아이들의 연령에 맞게 학습의 산을 작게 만들어 혼자서도 쉽게 넘을 수 있게 만듭니다. 때로는 작은 고난도 경험하게 하여 성취감도 맛보게 합니다. 그리고 아이들에게 실제로 적용해서 검증을 통해 차근차근 책을 만듭니다.

기적의 영어리딩 Level 1B

Miracle Series – Reading English

초판 1쇄 인쇄 • 2025년 11월 15일

지은이 • C2 Archive, 기적학습연구소

발행인 • 이종원
발행처 • (주)길벗스쿨
출판사 등록일 • 2025년 5월 28일 | **주소** • 서울시 마포구 월드컵로 10길 56(서교동) | **대표 전화** • 02)332-0931 | **팩스** • 02)323-0586
홈페이지 • www.gilbutschool.co.kr | **이메일** • gilbut@gilbut.co.kr

담당편집 • 이경희(natura@gilbut.co.kr), 최주연, 김예지, 유서현 | **기획** • 이경희, 김남희, 박민혜 | **영문 감수** • Ryan P. Lagace | **디자인** • 이현숙 | **제작** • 손일순
영업마케팅 • 문세연, 박선경, 구혜지, 박다슬 | **웹마케팅** • 박달님, 이재윤, 이지수, 나혜연 | **영업관리** • 정경화 | **독자지원** • 윤정아
전산편집 • 연디자인 | **삽화** • 주민정, 백정석, 박소현, 김보경 | **인쇄** • 영림인쇄 | **제본** • 영림제본 | **녹음** • 아람 멀티미디어

Photo Credits
해당 이미지는 Shutterstock.com의 라이선스 하에 사용되었습니다.
p.80 (Proonty) p.82 (Yuganov Konstantin, LightField Studios) p.83 (Thephotographer888) p.84 (Daniel Besic, Pixel-Shot)

ISBN 979-11-7467-045-8 64740 (길벗 도서번호 30612)
정가 17,000원

제 품 명 : 기적의 영어리딩 1B
제조사명 : 길벗스쿨
제조국명 : 대한민국
전화번호 : 02-332-0931
주 소 : 서울시 마포구 월드컵로 10길 56 (서교동)
제조년월 : 판권에 별도 표기
사용연령 : **8세 이상**
KC마크는 이 제품이 공통안전기준에 적합하였음을 의미합니다.

기적 영어 학습서

기본이 탄탄! 실전에서 척척!
유초등 필수 영어능력을 길러주는 코어 학습서

유아 영어

재미있는 액티비티가 가득한
4~6세를 위한 영어 워크북

4세 이상 | 5세 이상 | 6세 이상 | 6세 이상

파닉스 완성 프로그램

알파벳 음가 → 사이트워드
→ 읽기 연습까지!
리딩을 위한 탄탄한 기초 만들기

6세 이상 전 3권 | 1~3학년 | 1~3학년 전 3권

영어 단어

영어 실력의 가장 큰 바탕은 어휘력!
교과과정 필수 어휘 익히기

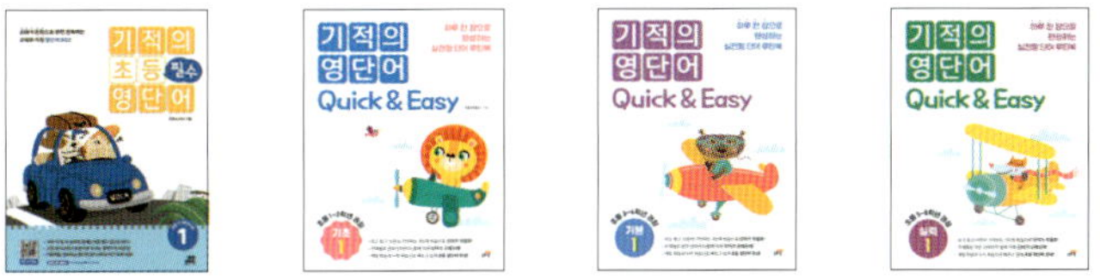

3학년 이상 전 2권 | 1~2학년 전 2권 | 3~4학년 전 2권 | 5~6학년 전 2권

영어 리딩

패턴 문장 리딩으로 시작해
정확한 해석을 위한 끊어 읽기까지!
탄탄한 독해 실력 쌓기

2~3학년 전 3권 | 3~4학년 전 3권 | 4~5학년 전 2권 | 5~6학년 전 2권 | 5~6학년 전 2권

영어 라이팅

저학년은 패턴 영작으로,
고학년은 5형식 문장 만들기 연습으로
튼튼한 영작 실력 완성

2학년 이상 전 4권 | 4학년 이상 전 5권 | 5학년 이상 전 2권 | 6학년 이상

영어일기

한 줄 쓰기부터 생활일기,
주제일기까지!
영어 글쓰기 실력을 키우는 시리즈

3학년 이상 | 4~5학년 | 5~6학년

영문법

중학 영어 대비, 영어 구사
정확성을 키워주는 영문법 학습

4~5학년 전 2권 | 5~6학년 전 3권 | 6학년 이상

초등 필수 영어 무작정 따라하기

초등 시기에 놓쳐서는 안 될 필수 학습은 바로 영어 교과서!
영어 교과서 5종의 핵심 내용을 쏙쏙 뽑아 한 권으로 압축 정리했습니다.
초등 과정의 필수학습으로 기초를 다져서 중학교 및 상위 학습의 단단한 토대가 되게 합니다.

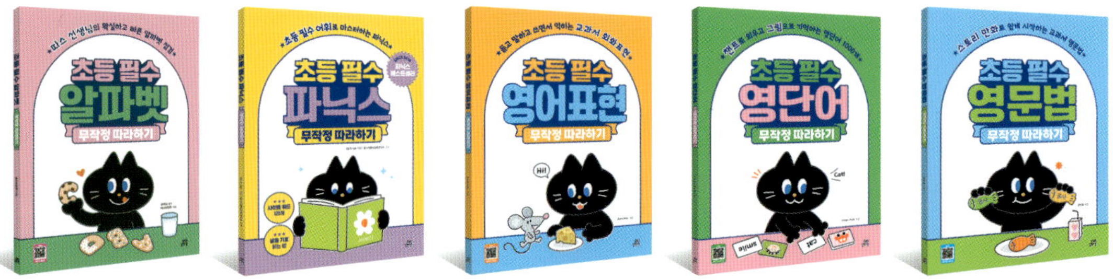

1~2학년 | 2~3학년 | 2~3학년 | 3학년 이상 | 4학년 이상

미국교과서 리딩

문제의 차이가 영어 실력의 차이! 논픽션 리딩에 강해지는 《미국교과서 READING》
논픽션 리딩에 가장 좋은 재료인 미국 교과과정의 주제를 담은 지문을 읽고, 독해력과
문제 해결력을 두루 향상시킬 수 있도록 구성한 단계별 리딩 프로그램

- **LEVEL 1** 준비 단계
- **LEVEL 2** 시작 단계
- **LEVEL 3** 정독 연습 단계
- **LEVEL 4** 독해 정확성 향상 단계
- **LEVEL 5** 독해 통합심화 단계

1B

리딩 첫 시작
AR 0.5~1.0

기적의 영어리딩 with 파닉스

Practice Book

(정답과 해석 포함)

길벗스쿨

기적의 영어리딩 1B

Practice Book

(정답과 해석 포함)

Unit 1 Behind the Curtains

Word

• 단어를 세 번씩 따라 쓰며 뜻과 철자를 익혀 보세요.

1 

bed 침대

2 

curtain 커튼

3 

monster 괴물

4 

pig 돼지

5 

scared 무서워하는

6 

spider 거미

Sentence

• 빈칸에 알맞은 단어를 써넣어 문장을 완성하세요.

1. "It's ______ for bed!"
   "잘 시간이야!"

2. Something is behind the ______s.
   커튼 뒤에 무엇인가 있어요.

3. Is it a red ______?
   빨간 거미인가요?

4. Is it a scary ______?
   무시무시한 괴물인가요?

5. I feel ______.
   나는 무서워요.

6. "Mom, can you ______ me?"
   "엄마, 저 좀 도와주실래요?"

7. Teddy is my bedtime ______.
   테디는 내 잠자리 친구예요.

curtain
scared
time
help
spider
monster
buddy

Unit 1 Behind the Curtains

Listening

• 잘 듣고 알맞은 단어에 동그라미 하세요.

P1.mp3

"It's time for (red / bed)!"

Look!
Something is behind the curtains.
What could it be?

Is it a red (spider / monster)?
Is it a big pig?

Is it a (scary / scared) monster?
I feel scared.

"Mom, can you (have / help) me?"
"Let's check together.
One, two, three – look!"

Oh, it's (Daddy / Teddy)!
Teddy is my bedtime buddy.

• 같은 소리를 가진 단어들끼리 모아 아래 표에 쓰세요.

bed daddy pig

big sled dig

Teddy buddy red

-ig	-ed	-dy

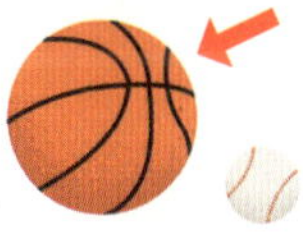		

Word

• 단어를 세 번씩 따라 쓰며 뜻과 철자를 익혀 보세요.

1 

candy 사탕

2 

fast 빠른

3 

lift 들어 올리다

4 

monkey 원숭이

5 

rocket 로켓

6 

seal 물개

• 빈칸에 알맞은 단어를 써넣어 문장을 완성하세요.

1. Dad is sweet like ______.
   아빠는 사탕처럼 달콤해요.

2. Dad is ______ like a bear.
   아빠는 곰처럼 힘이 세요.

3. He can ______ me up high!
   그는 저를 높이 들어 올릴 수 있어요!

4. Dad is funny like a ______.
   아빠는 원숭이처럼 웃겨요.

5. Dad is ______ like a rocket.
   아빠는 로켓처럼 빨라요.

6. Dad is cool like a ______.
   아빠는 물개처럼 멋져요.

7. He can ______ in the sea.
   그는 바다에서 수영을 할 수 있어요.

strong
swim
fast
lift
candy
seal
monkey

My Amazing Dad

Listening

• 잘 듣고 알맞은 단어에 동그라미 하세요.

P2.mp3

Dad is (sweet / strong) like candy.
He gives me a big (bug / hug).

Dad is strong like a (bear / pear).
He can lift me up high!

Dad is (fast / funny) like a monkey.
He can make a funny face.

Dad is fast like a rocket.
He wins every (lace / race).

Dad is cool like a (meal / seal).
He can swim in the sea.

I love my dad so much.
He is the (best / nest)!

• 같은 소리를 가진 단어들끼리 모아 아래 표에 쓰세요.

face race nest

fast read best

seal lace sea

-st

-ace

-ea-

• 단어를 세 번씩 따라 쓰며 뜻과 철자를 익혀 보세요.

1

bike 자전거

2

hold (손으로) 잡고 있다

3

new 새, 새로 산

4

path 길

5

ride (자전거 등을) 타기, 타다

6

shout 큰 소리로 말하다, 외치다

Sentence

• 빈칸에 알맞은 단어를 써넣어 문장을 완성하세요.

1. I have a shiny new ______.
   나는 새로 산 반짝이는 자전거를 가지고 있어요.

2. It's a ______ gift from Dad.
   그건 아빠가 내 생일 선물로 주신 거예요.

3. We're both ______.
   아빠랑 나 모두 신이 나요.

4. The ______ is wide.
   길이 넓어요.

5. I feel a little ______.
   나는 조금 긴장돼요.

6. "______ on tight for me," I say.
   "나를 꼭 잡아 주세요," 내가 말해요.

7. "Are you still holding on?" I ______.
   "지금도 잡고 있어요?" 내가 소리쳐요.

path
hold
bike
birthday
excited
shout
nervous

My First Ride

Listening

• 잘 듣고 알맞은 단어에 동그라미 하세요.

P3.mp3

I have a shiny (old / new) bike.
It's a birthday gift from Dad.

We get our bikes.
Dad will (hold / help) me ride.
We're both (excited / exciting).

The path is (narrow / wide).
I feel a little nervous.

"Hold on (tight / sight) for me," I say.
"Okay," Dad says.

"Are you still holding on?"
I (shout / say).

I look back.
I'm riding all by myself!

• 같은 소리를 가진 단어들끼리 모아 아래 표에 쓰세요.

ride   ship   wide

shiny   hide   path

tooth   shout   both

sh-

-th

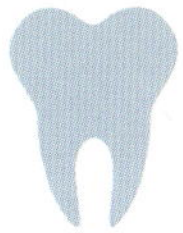

-ide

Unit 4 Maybe Next Time!

Word

• 단어를 세 번씩 따라 쓰며 뜻과 철자를 익혀 보세요.

1 

bored 지루해하는

2 

hurt 아프다

3 

mess 엉망인 상태

4 

play 놀다

5 

read 읽다, 읽어주다

6 

tidy up ~을 정리하다

Sentence

• 빈칸에 알맞은 단어를 써넣어 문장을 완성하세요.

1. I'm ______ .
   나는 지루해요.

2. I want to ______ .
   나는 놀고 싶어요.

3. I ______ it's going to rain.
   내가 추측하기엔 곧 비가 올 거 같아.

4. ______ me a story, Mom.
   책 읽어 주세요, 엄마.

5. My head ______ s.
   난 머리가 아프구나.

6. What a ______ !
   어쩜 이렇게 난장판이야!

7. It's time to ______ !
   이제 정리할 시간이야!

play
read
tidy up
guess
mess
bored
hurt

Unit 4 **Maybe Next Time!** Listening

• 잘 듣고 알맞은 단어에 동그라미 하세요.

P4.mp3

Alex: I'm bored.

I want to (play / read).

Alex: Let's play (soccer / basketball), Dad.

Dad: I guess it's going to rain.

Maybe next time!

Alex: Read me a (story / book), Mom.

Mom: My head hurts.

Maybe next time!

Alex: Ta-da! I have slime and a (train / car).

Emma: Maybe next time!

Alex: Fine, I'll just play all by myself.

Family: What a (miss / mess)!

It's time to tidy up!

Alex: Maybe next time!

- 같은 소리를 가진 단어들끼리 모아 아래 표에 쓰세요.

guess rain train

lime time dress

slime chain mess

-ess	-ime	-ain

Unit 5 Day and Night

Word

• 단어를 세 번씩 따라 쓰며 뜻과 철자를 익혀 보세요.

1

morning 아침

2

night 밤

3

owl 올빼미

4

sleep (잠을) 자다

5

turn off (전기 등을) 끄다

6

wake up (잠에서) 깨다, 깨우다

Sentence

• 빈칸에 알맞은 단어를 써넣어 문장을 완성하세요.

1. The sun comes out in the ______ .
   해는 아침에 떠올라요.

2. Birds ______ me up.
   새들이 나를 깨워줘요.

3. The moon comes out at ______ .
   달은 밤에 떠올라요.

4. It gets ______ .
   날이 캄캄해져요.

5. Ben goes to ______ .
   벤은 잠을 자러 가요.

6. I ______ the light.
   나는 불을 꺼요.

7. ______ s hoot at night.
   올빼미들은 밤에 울어요.

dark
owl
night
wake
turn off
sleep
morning

Unit 5 # Day and Night

Listening

• 잘 듣고 알맞은 단어에 동그라미 하세요.

P5.mp3

• During the Day

The (moon / sun) comes out in the morning.
It gets bright.

Birds (wake / sleep) me up.

Dad goes to (school / work).
I go to (school / work).

• At Night

The moon comes out at (morning / night).
It gets dark.

Ben goes to sleep.
And I go to sleep, too.
I (tune / turn) off the light.

Owls hoot at (noon / night).
Aren't you sleepy, Mr. Owl?

● 같은 소리를 가진 단어들끼리 모아 아래 표에 쓰세요.

fight light spoon

moon night

school bright food

-ight

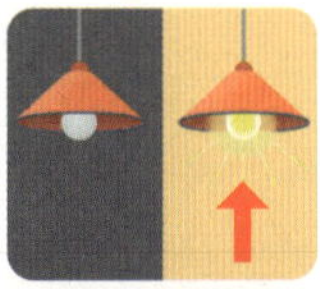

-oo-

Unit 6 The Three Little Pigs Word

• 단어를 세 번씩 따라 쓰며 뜻과 철자를 익혀 보세요.

1 

blow (입으로) 불다

2 

brick 벽돌

3 

build (건물을) 짓다

4 

house 집

5 

stick 나뭇가지, 막대기

6 

straw 짚, 지푸라기

Sentence

• 빈칸에 알맞은 단어를 써넣어 문장을 완성하세요.

1 "We're great ______ s," they say.
"우리는 훌륭한 건축가들이에요." 그들이 말해요.

2 The first pig builds a ______ house.
첫째 돼지는 지푸라기 집을 지어요.

3 The second pig builds a ______ house.
둘째 돼지는 나뭇가지 집을 지어요.

4 The third pig builds a ______ house.
셋째 돼지는 벽돌 집을 지어요.

5 The ______ blows the straw house away.
늑대가 지푸라기 집을 불어 날려 버려요.

6 The wolf cannot ______ the brick house down.
늑대는 벽돌 집을 불어 무너뜨리지 못해요.

7 The three little pigs dance in the dirt and ______ . 아기 돼지 삼 형제는 흙바람과 먼지 속에서 춤을 춰요.

straw
blow
builder
wolf
brick
stick
dust

Unit 6 The Three Little Pigs Listening

• 잘 듣고 알맞은 단어에 동그라미 하세요.

P6.mp3

The three (big / little) pigs live in a town.
"We're great (builders / buildings)," they say.

The first pig builds a (stick / straw) house.
The second pig builds a (stick / straw) house.

The third pig builds a brick house.
It is thick and (weak / strong).

"Knock, knock! Let me in."
The wolf (flows / blows) the straw house away.

"Knock, knock! Let me in."
The wolf blows the stick house away.

The wolf (can / cannot) blow the
brick house down.
The three little pigs dance
in the dirt and dust.

• 같은 소리를 가진 단어들끼리 모아 아래 표에 쓰세요.

girl dirt brick

first stick

kick thick third

-ick

-ir-

Practice Book 정답

Unit 1

p.3 Sentence

• 빈칸에 알맞은 단어를 써넣어 문장을 완성하세요.

1. "It's time for bed!"
2. Something is behind the curtain.
3. Is it a red spider?
4. Is it a scary monster?
5. I feel scared.
6. "Mom, can you help me?"
7. Teddy is my bedtime buddy.

curtain / scared / time / help / spider / monster / buddy

p.4 Unit 1 Behind the Curtains — Listening

• 잘 듣고 알맞은 단어에 동그라미 하세요.

"It's time for (red / bed)!" — bed
Look!
Something is behind the curtains.
What could it be?
Is it a red (spider / monster)? — spider
Is it a big pig?
Is it a (scary / scared) monster? — scary
I feel scared.
"Mom, can you (have / help) me? — help
"Let's check together.
One, two, three – look!"
Oh, it's (Daddy / Teddy)! — Teddy
Teddy is my bedtime buddy.

p.5 Phonics

• 같은 소리를 가진 단어들끼리 모아 아래 표에 쓰세요.

bed, daddy, pig, big, sled, dig, Teddy, buddy, red

-ig	-ed	-dy
pig	bed	buddy
big	red	Teddy
dig	sled	daddy

Unit 2

p.7 Sentence

• 빈칸에 알맞은 단어를 써넣어 문장을 완성하세요.

1. Dad is sweet like candy.
2. Dad is strong like a bear.
3. He can lift me up high!
4. Dad is funny like a monkey.
5. Dad is fast like a rocket.
6. Dad is cool like a seal.
7. He can swim in the sea.

strong / swim / fast / lift / candy / seal / monkey

p.8 Unit 2 My Amazing Dad — Listening

• 잘 듣고 알맞은 단어에 동그라미 하세요.

Dad is (sweet / strong) like candy. — sweet
He gives me a big (bug / hug). — hug
Dad is strong like a (bear / pear). — bear
He can lift me up high!
Dad is (fast / funny) like a monkey. — funny
He can make a funny face.
Dad is fast like a rocket.
He wins every (lace / race). — race
Dad is cool like a (meal / seal). — seal
He can swim in the sea.
I love my dad so much.
He is the (best / nest)! — best

p.9 Phonics

• 같은 소리를 가진 단어들끼리 모아 아래 표에 쓰세요.

face, race, nest, fast, read, best, seal, lace, sea

-st	-ace	-ea-
fast	face	seal
best	race	sea
nest	lace	read

Unit 3

p.11 Sentence

• 빈칸에 알맞은 단어를 써넣어 문장을 완성하세요.

1. I have a shiny new bike.
2. It's a birthday gift from Dad.
3. We're both excited.
4. The path is wide.
5. I feel a little nervous.
6. "Hold on tight for me," I say.
7. "Are you still holding on?" I shout.

path / hold / bike / birthday / excited / shout / nervous

p.12 Unit 3 My First Ride — Listening

• 잘 듣고 알맞은 단어에 동그라미 하세요.

I have a shiny (old / new) bike. — new
It's a birthday gift from Dad.
We get our bikes.
Dad will (hold / help) me ride. — help
We're both (excited / exciting). — excited
The path is (narrow / wide). — wide
I feel a little nervous.
"Hold on (tight / sight) for me," I say. — tight
"Okay," Dad says.
"Are you still holding on?"
I (shout / say). — shout
I look back.
I'm riding all by myself!

p.13 Phonics

• 같은 소리를 가진 단어들끼리 모아 아래 표에 쓰세요.

ride, ship, wide, shiny, hide, path, tooth, shout, both

sh-	-th	-ide
shiny	both	ride
shout	path	wide
ship	tooth	hide

Unit 4

p.15

Sentence

1. I'm **bored**.
2. I want to **play**.
3. I **guess** it's going to rain.
4. **Read** me a story, Mom.
5. My head **hurt**s.
6. What a **mess**!
7. It's time to **tidy up**!

play / read / tidy up / guess / mess / bored / hurt

Unit 4 15

p.16

Maybe Next Time! — Listening

Alex: I'm bored.
I want to (play / read). **play**

Alex: Let's play (soccer / basketball), Dad. **soccer**

Dad: I guess it's going to rain.
Maybe next time!

Alex: Read me a (story / book), Mom. **story**

Mom: My head hurts.
Maybe next time!

Alex: Ta-da! I have slime and a (train / car). **train**

Emma: Maybe next time!

Alex: Fine. I'll just play all by myself.

Family: What a (miss / mess)! **mess**
It's time to tidy up!

Alex: Maybe next time!

16

p.17

Phonics

guess, rain, train, lime, time, dress, slime, chain, mess

-ess	-ime	-ain
mess	slime	train
guess	time	rain
dress	lime	chain

Unit 4 17

Unit 5

p.19

Sentence

1. The sun comes out in the **morning**.
2. Birds **wake** me up.
3. The moon comes out at **night**.
4. It gets **dark**.
5. Ben goes to **sleep**.
6. I **turn off** the light.
7. **Owl**s hoot at night.

dark / owl / night / wake / turn off / sleep / morning

Unit 5 19

p.20

Day and Night — Listening

• During the Day

The (moon / sun) comes out in the morning. **sun**
It gets bright.

Birds (wake / sleep) me up. **wake**

Dad goes to (school / work). **work**
I go to (school / work). **school**

• At Night

The moon comes out at (morning / night). **night**
It gets dark.

Ben goes to sleep.
And I go to sleep, too.
I (tune / turn) off the light. **turn**

Owls hoot at (noon / night). **night**
Aren't you sleepy, Mr. Owl?

20

p.21

Phonics

fight, light, spoon, moon, night, school, bright, food

-ight	-oo-
light	spoon
bright	moon
night	school
fight	food

Unit 5 21

Unit 6

p.23

Sentence

1. "We're great **builder**s," they say.
2. The first pig builds a **straw** house.
3. The second pig builds a **stick** house.
4. The third pig builds a **brick** house.
5. The **wolf** blows the straw house away.
6. The wolf cannot **blow** the brick house down.
7. The three little pigs dance in the dirt and **dust**.

straw / blow / builder / wolf / brick / stick / dust

Unit 6 23

p.24

The Three Little Pigs — Listening

The three (big / little) pigs live in a town. **little**
"We're great (builders / buildings)," they say. **builders**

The first pig builds a (stick / straw) house. **straw**
The second pig builds a (stick / straw) house. **stick**

The third pig builds a brick house.
It is thick and (weak / strong). **strong**

"Knock, knock! Let me in."
The wolf (flows / blows) the straw house away. **blows**

"Knock, knock! Let me in."
The wolf blows the stick house away.

The wolf (can / cannot) blow the brick house down. **cannot**
The three little pigs dance in the dirt and dust.

24

p.25

Phonics

girl, dirt, brick, first, stick, kick, thick, third

-ick	-ir-
thick	dirt
brick	first
stick	third
kick	girl

Unit 6 25

Story Reading

p.14

"잘 시간이야!"

p.15

봐요!
커튼 뒤에 무언가 있어요.
그건 무엇일까요?

p.16

빨간 거미인가요?
커다란 돼지인가요?

p.17

무시무시한 괴물인가요?
나는 무서워요.

p.18

"엄마, 저 좀 도와주실래요?"
"같이 확인해 보자!
하나, 둘, 셋 – 봐!"

p.19

아, 그건 테디네요!
테디는 내 잠자리 친구예요.

Story Words

time 시간, 때	behind ~ 뒤에	curtain 커튼	spider 거미
look 바라보다	monster 괴물	scared 무서워하는	check 점검하다, 확인하다

Phonics Words

-ed	bed 침대	red 빨간, 붉은	sled 썰매
-ig	big 큰	pig 돼지	dig (구멍 등을) 파다
-dy	Teddy 테디(곰 인형)	buddy 친구	daddy 아빠

Answers

p.13

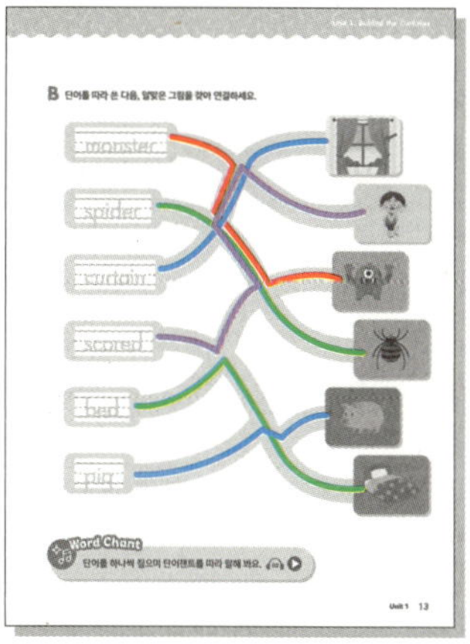

p.20

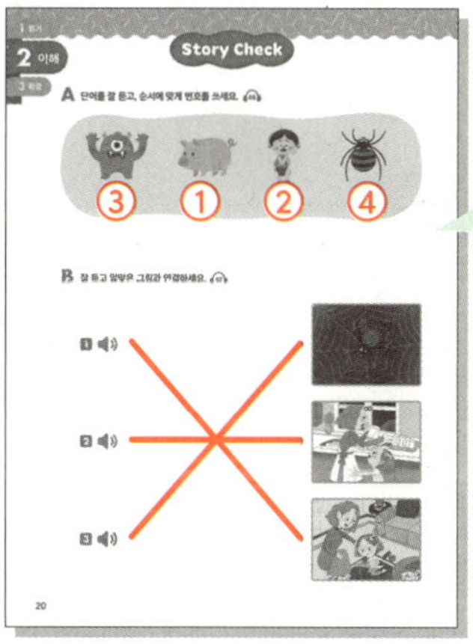

script

A

1. pig
2. scared
3. monster
4. spider

B

1. It's time for bed!
2. Mom, can you help me?
3. Is it a red spider?

p.21

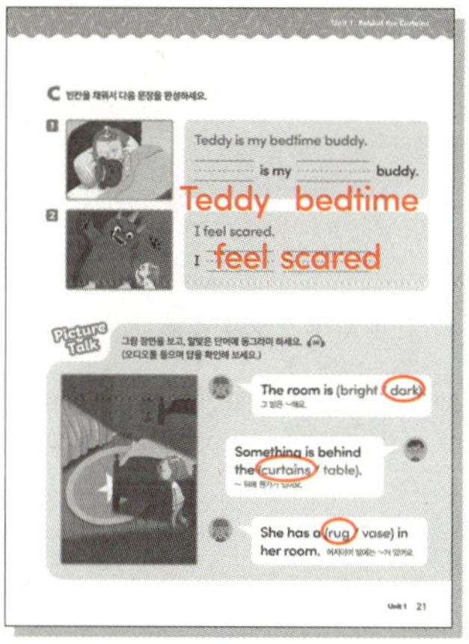

p.22

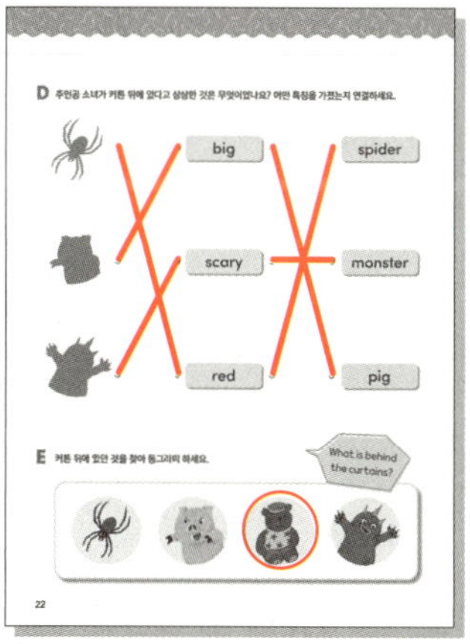

p.23

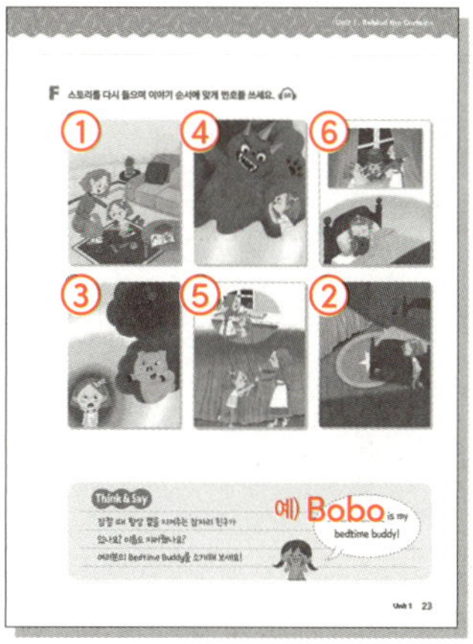

p.24

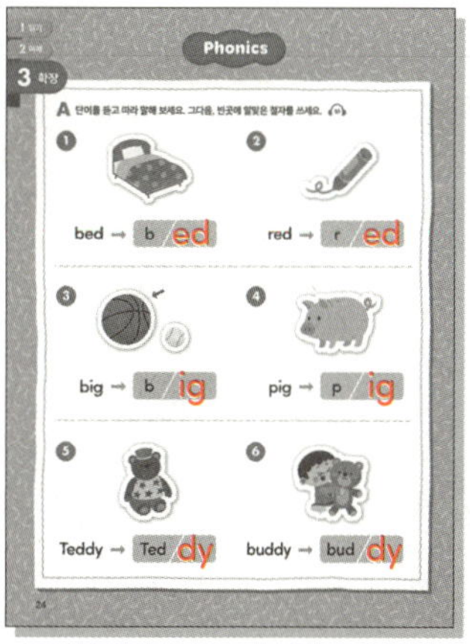

p.25

Story Reading

p.30

아빠는 사탕처럼 달콤해요.
아빠는 나를 꼭 안아 주세요.

p.31

아빠는 곰처럼 힘이 세요.
아빠는 저를 높이 들어 올릴 수 있어요!

p.32

아빠는 원숭이처럼 웃겨요.
아빠는 웃긴 표정을 지을 수 있어요.

p.33

아빠는 로켓처럼 빨라요.
아빠는 모든 경주에서 이겨요.

p.34

아빠는 물개처럼 멋져요.
아빠는 바다에서 수영을 할 수 있어요.

p.35

나는 아빠를 아주 많이 사랑해요.
아빠는 최고예요!

Story Words

sweet 달콤한	candy 사탕	strong 강한	lift 들어 올리다
monkey 원숭이	funny 우스운, 이상한	rocket 로켓	swim 수영하다

Phonics Words

-ace	race 경주, 달리기	face 얼굴	lace 신발 끈
-ea-	seal 물개	sea 바다	read 읽다
-st	fast 빠른	best 최고의	nest (새의) 둥지

Answers

p.29

p.36

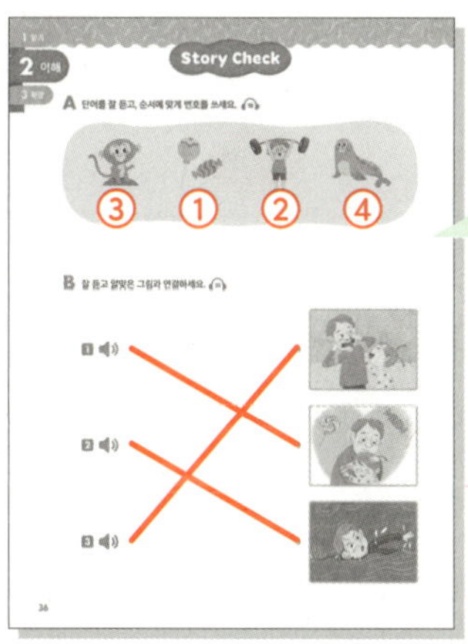

script

A
1. candy 2. lift
3. monkey 4. seal

B
1. He gives me a big hug.
2. He can swim in the sea.
3. Dad is funny like a monkey.

p.37

p.38

p.39

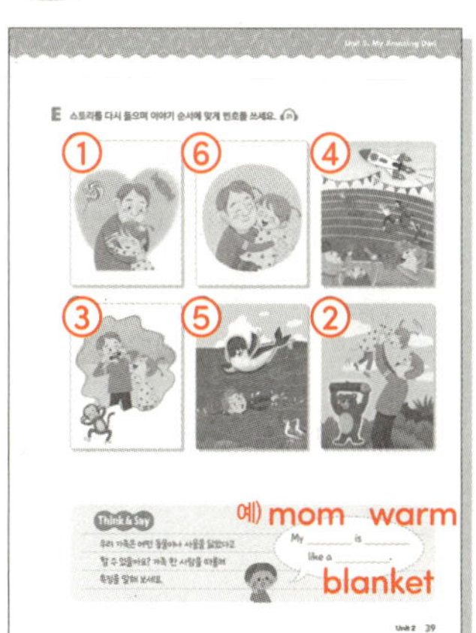

p.40

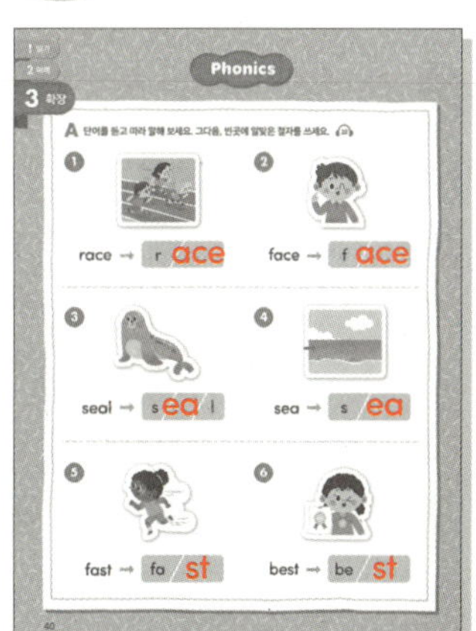

p.41

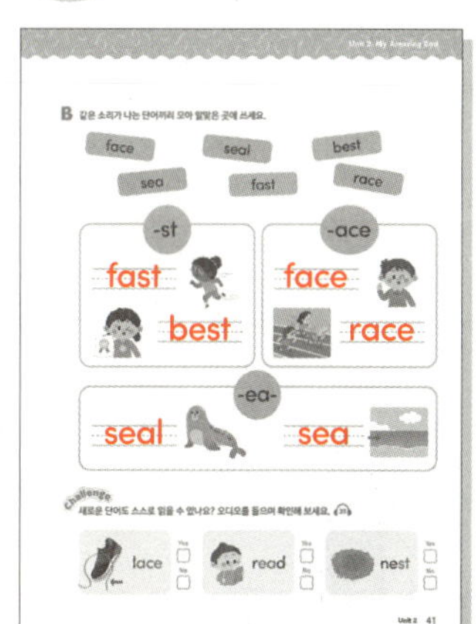

Unit 3 # My First Ride 나의 첫 자전거 타기

Story Reading

p.46

나는 반짝이는 새 자전거가 있어요.
그건 아빠가 주신 생일 선물이에요.

p.47

우리는 자전거를 챙겨요.
아빠는 내가 자전거 타는 것을 도와줄 거예요.
우리 둘 다 신이 나요.

p.48

길이 넓어요.
나는 조금 긴장돼요.

p.49

"나를 꼭 잡아 주세요." 내가 말해요.
"알았어," 아빠가 말해요.

Tip a little: 약간, 조금
nervous: 긴장되는

p.50

"지금도 잡고 있어요?" 내가 소리쳐요.

p.51

나는 뒤를 돌아봐요.
나는 혼자서 자전거를 타고 있어요!

Tip all by myself: (남의 도움 없이) 혼자

Story Words

shiny 반짝거리는	new 새, 새로 산	bike 자전거	gift 선물
nervous 긴장되는	tight 꽉, 단단히	excited 신이 난	hold (손으로) 잡고 있다

Phonics Words

-ide	ride (자전거 등을) 타다, 타기	wide 넓은	hide 숨다, 숨기다
-th	path 길	both 둘 다(의)	tooth 이, 이빨
sh-	shiny 반짝거리는	shout 큰 소리로 말하다, 외치다	ship 배

Answers

p.45

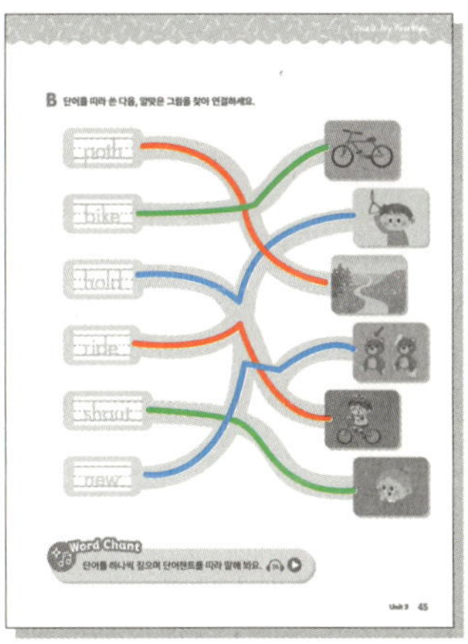

p.52

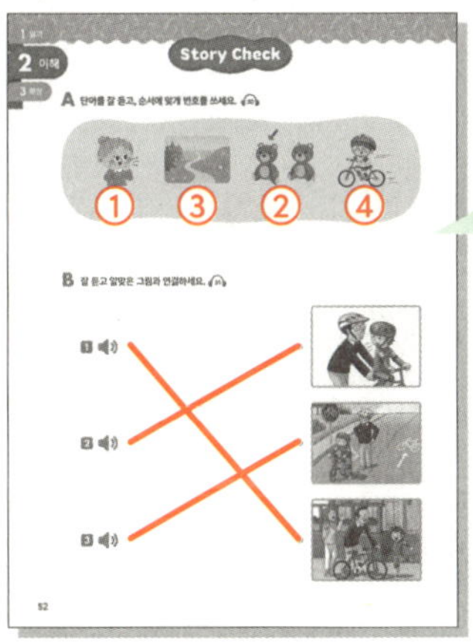

script
A
1. shout 2. new
3. path 4. ride

B
1. It's a birthday gift from Dad.
2. Hold on tight for me.
3. I feel a little nervous.

p.53

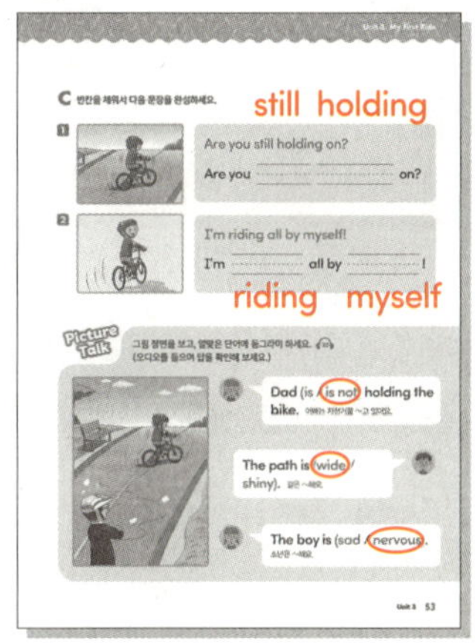

p.54

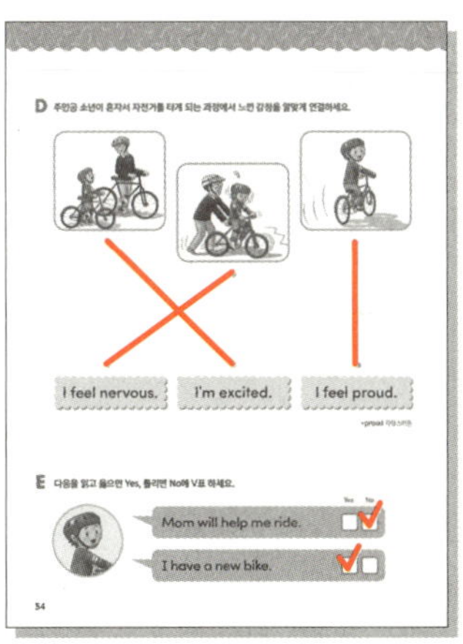

p.55

p.56

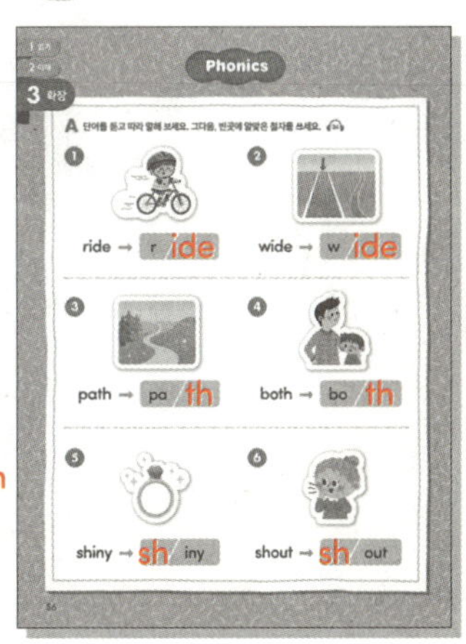

p.57

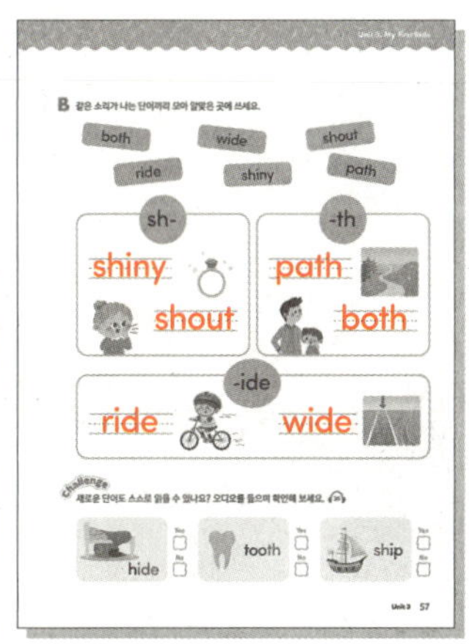

Unit 4 Maybe Next Time! 다음에 하자!

Story Reading

p.66

나: 나는 지루해.
나는 놀고 싶어.

p.67

나: 같이 축구해요, 아빠.
아빠: 내가 추측하기엔 곧 비가 올 거 같아.
다음에 하자!

p.68

나: 책 읽어주세요, 엄마.
엄마: 난 머리가 아프구나.
다음에 하자!

p.69

나: 짜잔! 나 슬라임이랑 기차 있어.
누나: 다음에 하자!

p.70

나: 좋아, 그냥 나 혼자 놀 거야.
가족: 어쩜 이렇게 난장판이야!
이제 정리할 시간이야!

p.71

나: 다음에 할게요!

Story Words

bored 지루해하는	play 놀다	soccer 축구	read 읽다, 읽어주다
hurt 아프다	story 이야기	next 다음의	tidy up ~을 정리하다

Phonics Words

-ime	time 시간	slime 슬라임, 끈적한 물질	lime 라임
-ain	rain 비가 오다, 비	train 기차	chain 사슬
-ess	guess 추측하다	mess 엉망인 상태	dress 드레스, 원피스

Answers

p.65

p.72

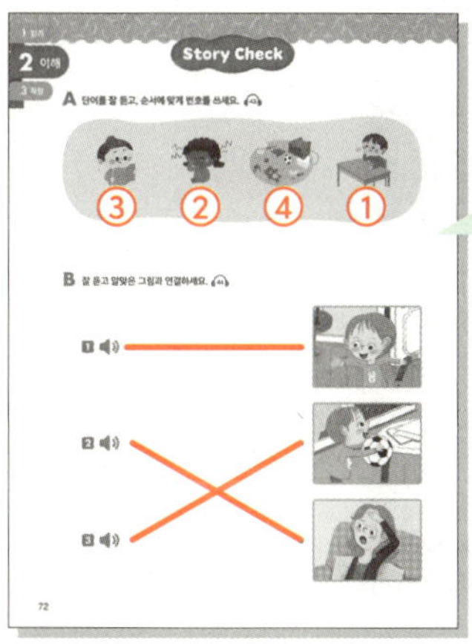

script

A

1. bored
2. hurt
3. read
4. mess

B

1. I have slime and a train.
2. My head hurts.
3. Let's play soccer, Dad.

p.73

p.74

p.75

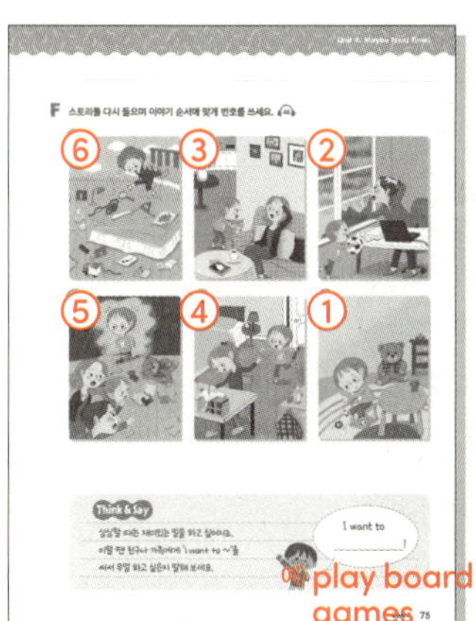

p.76

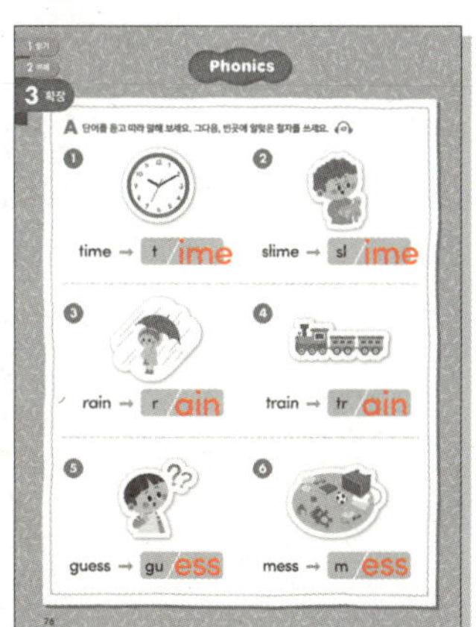

p.77

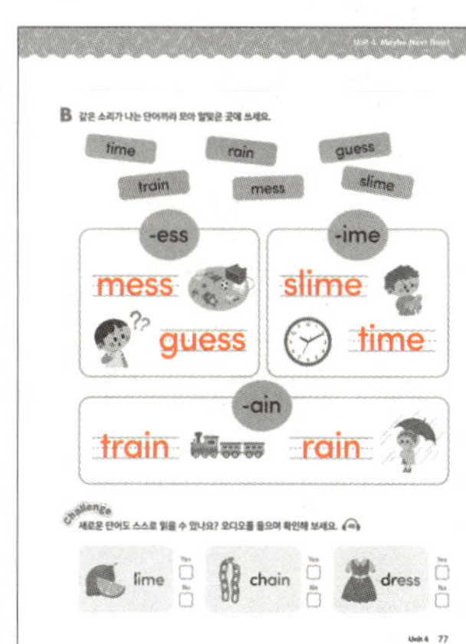

Unit 5

Day and Night 낮과 밤

Story Reading

p.82

● **낮 동안**

아침에 해가 나와요.
날이 밝아져요.

p.83

“짹짹!”
새들이 나를 깨워요.

p.84

아빠는 직장에 가요.
나는 학교에 가요.

p.85

● **밤에**

밤에 달이 나와요.
날이 어두워져요.

p.86

벤은 잠을 자러 가요.
나도 잠을 자러 가요.
나는 불을 꺼요.

p.87

“부엉, 부엉!”
부엉이들은 밤에 울어요.
부엉이 아저씨, 안 졸리세요?

Tip hoot: (부엉이가) 부엉부엉 하다

Story Words

morning 아침	bird 새	wake up (잠에서) 깨다, 깨우다	work 일하다
dark 어두운	sleep (잠을) 자다	turn off (전기 등을) 끄다	owl 올빼미

Phonics Words

-ight	bright 밝은	night 밤	light 빛, 밝은	fight 싸우다
-oo-	school 학교	spoon 숟가락	moon 달	food 음식

Answers

p.81

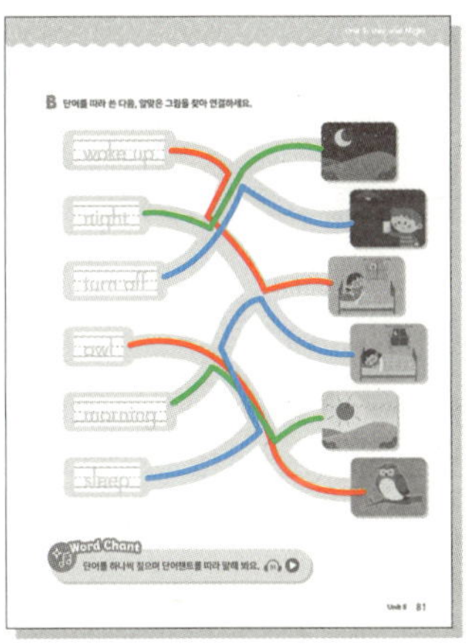

p.88

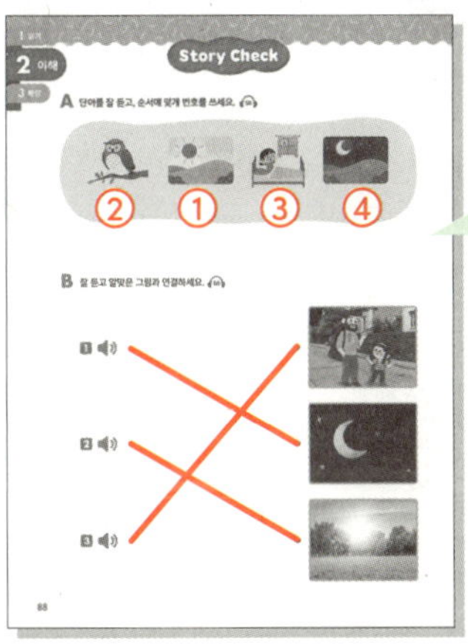

script

A

1. morning 2. owl
3. wake up 4. night

B

1. The moon comes out at night.
2. The sun comes out in the morning.
3. Dad goes to work.

p.89

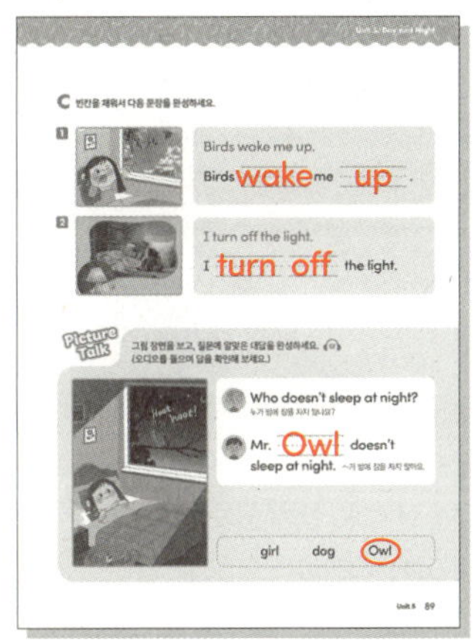

p.90

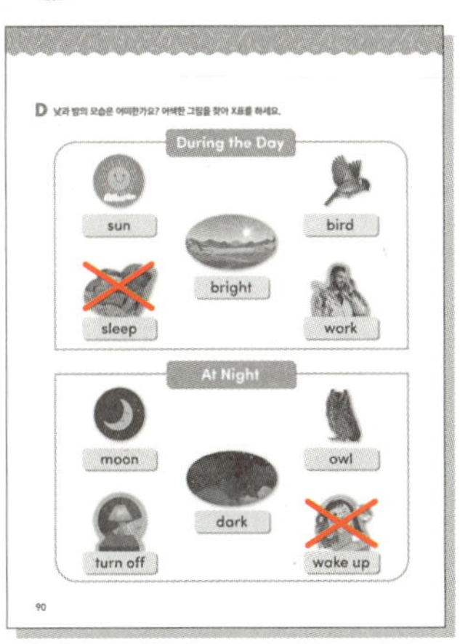

p.91

p.92

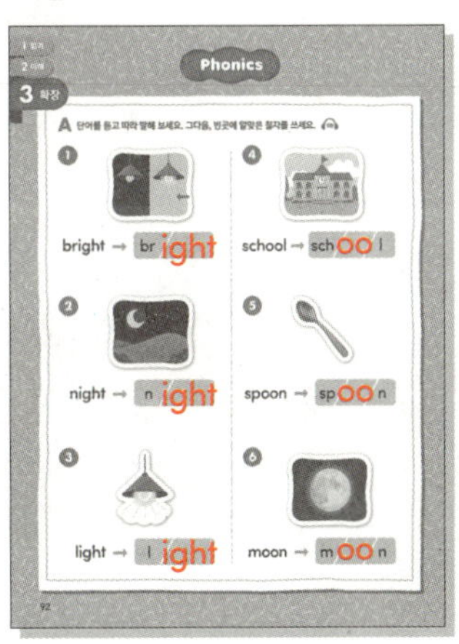

p.93

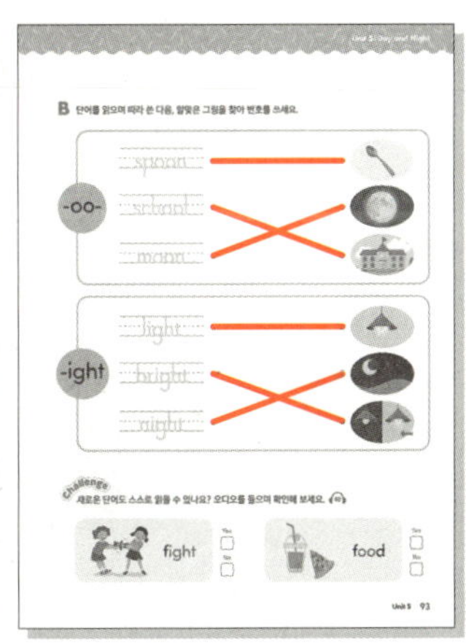

Unit 6 **The Three Little Pig** 아기 돼지 삼형제

Story Reading

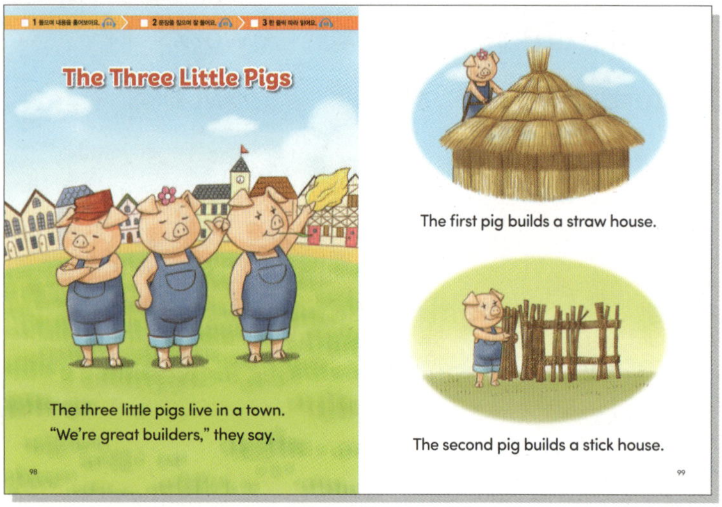

p.98

아기 돼지 삼형제는 작은 도시에 살고 있어요.
"우리는 훌륭한 건축가들이에요." 그들이 말해요.

p.99

첫째 돼지는 지푸라기 집을 지어요.
둘째 돼지는 나뭇가지 집을 지어요.

p.100

셋째 돼지는 벽돌 집을 지어요.
그것은 두껍고 튼튼해요.

p.101

"똑똑! 날 들여보내."
늑대가 지푸라기 집을 불어 날려버려요.

Tip one, two, three처럼 개수를 세는 수는 '기수'라 하고, first, second, third처럼 순서를 세는 수는 '서수'라고 해요.

p.102

"똑똑! 날 들여보내 줘."
늑대가 나뭇가지 집을 불어 날려버려요.

p.103

늑대는 벽돌 집을 불어 무너뜨리지 못해요.
아기 돼지 삼형제는 흙바람과 먼지 속에서 춤을 춰요.

Story Words

town 작은 도시, 시내	build (건물을) 짓다	straw 짚, 지푸라기	house 집
stick 나뭇가지, 막대기	wolf 늑대	blow (입으로) 불다	dance 춤추다

Phonics Words

-ick	stick 나뭇가지, 막대기	brick 벽돌	thick 두꺼운	kick (발로) 차다
-ir-	third 셋째의	first 첫째의	dirt 흙, 먼지	girl 여자아이

Answers

p.97

p.104

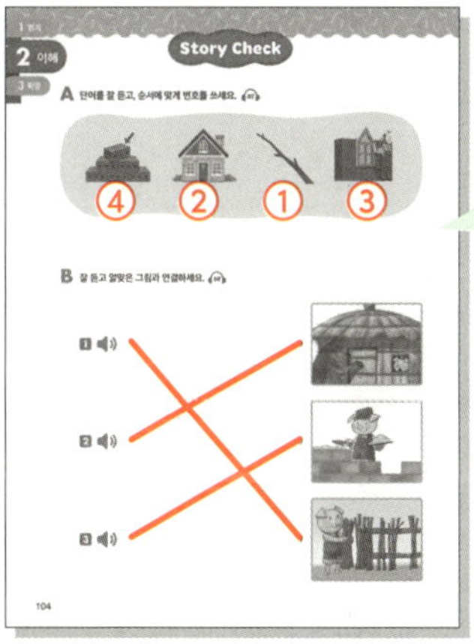

script

A

1. stick 2. house
3. build 4. brick

B

1. The second pig builds a stick house.
2. "Knock, knock! Let me in."
3. The third pig builds a brick house.

p.105

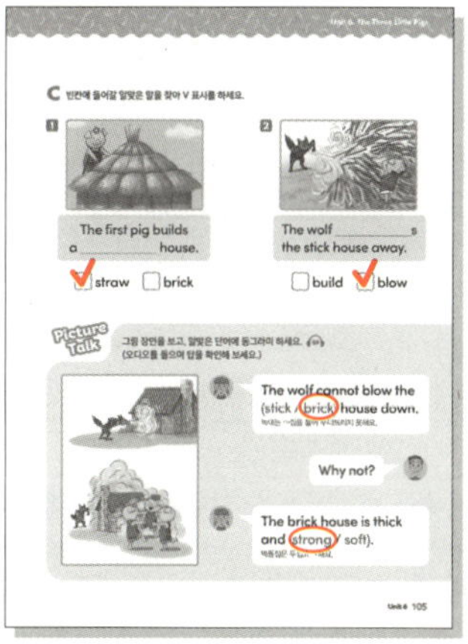

p.106

p.107

p.108

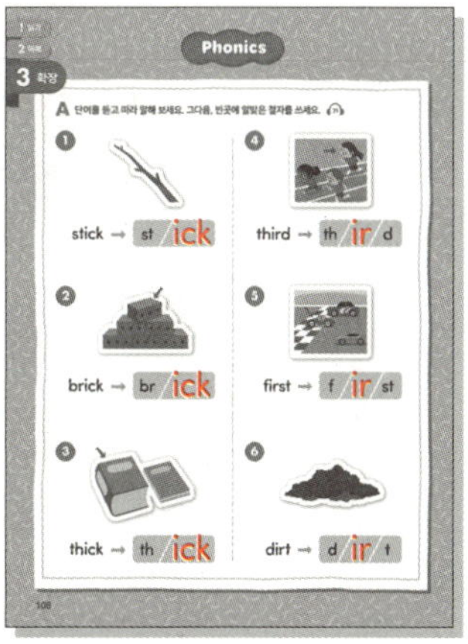

p.109

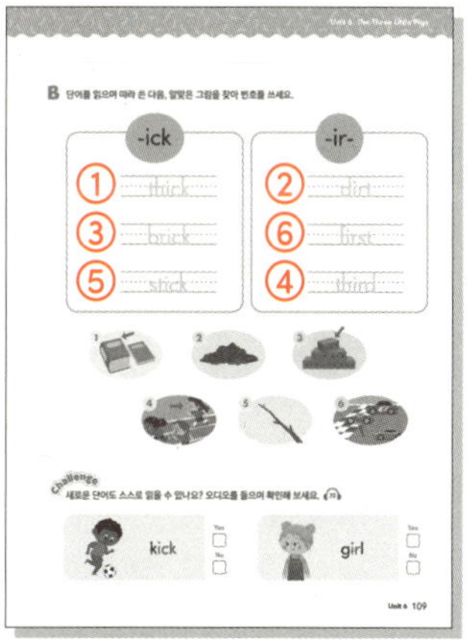

Review Test 정답

p.59

Review Test 1 — Unit 1~3

Words 그림을 보고 알맞은 단어에 V 표시를 하세요. (/ 10)

1. [x] seal [ ] monkey
2. [ ] bed [x] curtain
3. [ ] sea [x] path
4. [x] rocket [ ] bike
5. [ ] bear [x] pig
6. [ ] old [x] new
7. [x] monster [ ] spider
8. [ ] wide [x] fast
9. [x] hold [ ] ride
10. [x] bike [ ] box

Review Test 1 59

p.60

Comprehension A 다음을 읽고 알맞은 그림에 V 표시를 하세요. (/ 6)

1. sweet like candy — second picture ✓
2. a scary monster — first picture ✓
3. behind the curtains — second picture ✓
4. a shiny new bike — first picture ✓
5. make a funny face — second picture ✓
6. help me ride — second picture ✓

60

p.61

Comprehension B 빈칸에 들어갈 알맞은 단어에 V 표시를 하세요. (/ 5)

1. We're both ______. [x] excited [ ] nervous
2. Dad is funny like a ______. [ ] seal [x] monkey
3. The ______ is wide. [ ] bike [x] path
4. Teddy is my bedtime ______. [ ] daddy [x] buddy
5. Dad can ______ me up high! [x] lift [ ] swim

Review Test 1 61

p.62

Phonics 단어를 잘 듣고 알맞은 것에 동그라미 한 뒤, 그림과 연결하세요. (/ 8)

1. race / (face)
2. (red) / bed
3. (best) / fast
4. (ride) / wide
5. path / (both)
6. (buddy) / Teddy
7. (shout) / shiny
8. pig / (big)

62

p.111

Review Test 2 — Unit 4~6

Words 그림을 보고 알맞은 단어에 V 표시를 하세요. (/ 10)

1. [x] mess [ ] dust
2. [x] house [ ] train
3. [ ] sleep [x] wake up
4. [x] turn off [ ] tidy up
5. [x] brick [ ] stick
6. [ ] read [x] hurt
7. [ ] blow [x] play
8. [ ] wake up [x] sleep
9. [x] morning [ ] night
10. [ ] stick [x] straw

Review Test 2 111

p.112

Comprehension A 다음을 읽고 알맞은 그림에 V 표시를 하세요. (/ 6)

1. turn off the light — second picture ✓
2. a stick house — first picture ✓
3. blow away — second picture ✓
4. I'm bored. — second picture ✓
5. It gets dark. — second picture ✓
6. go to sleep — second picture ✓

112

p.113

Comprehension B 빈칸에 들어갈 알맞은 단어에 V 표시를 하세요. (/ 5)

1. ______ hoot at night. [ ] Pigs [x] Owls
2. The first pig ______ a straw house. [x] builds [ ] blows
3. "Let's ______ soccer." [ ] read [x] play
4. "My ______ hurts." [ ] eyes [x] head
5. "What a ______!" [ ] clean [x] mess

Review Test 2 113

p.114

Phonics 단어를 잘 듣고 알맞은 것에 동그라미 한 뒤, 그림과 연결하세요. (/ 8)

1. (rain) / train
2. stick / (brick)
3. time / (slime)
4. (thick) / stick
5. (night) / light
6. school / (spoon)
7. mess / (guess)
8. (dirt) / third

114

"방법이 다르면 결과가 달라집니다"

리딩 실력을 껑충 키우는

기적만의 3-Step 완전학습

기적의 영어리딩
* 전문가가 설계한 6단계 리딩 프로그램으로 빈틈없는 영어 문해력 완성!
이해한 내용을 문장으로 쓸 수 있어요.
Level 6
with 서술형 영작
: 읽은 내용을 정리하는 표현력 기르기
중요한 내용을 찾고 요약할 수 있어요.
Level 5
with 문법
: 글을 논리적으로 이해하여 핵심 파악하기
글의 구조와 문장의 어순에 익숙해져요.
Level 4
with 문장 구조
: 다양한 글감을 읽으며 문장 구성력 키우기
문장 패턴에 익숙해져 읽고 이해하기가 쉬워져요.
Level 3
with 문장 패턴
: 교과서 필수 문형과 함께 문장 이해 연습
짧은 문장을 읽고 이해하는 자신감이 붙어요.
Level 2
with 주제 어휘
: 기초 문형과 어휘를 익히며 읽기 유창성 높이기
문자를 소리 내어 읽을 수 있어요.
Level 1
with 파닉스
: 문자 해독력을 높이는 리딩 연습